Fishing Boats
and their Equipment

Fishing Boats and their Equipment

Dag Pike

Fishing News Books

Published by
Fishing News Books Ltd
1 Long Garden Walk
Farnham, Surrey
England

British Library CIP data
Pike, Dag
    Fishing Boats and their Equipment
    1. Fishing Boats
    I. Title
    623.82'8   VM431

ISBN 0 85238 090 9

Typeset by Inforum Ltd, Portsmouth
Printed and bound in Great Britain by
The Pitman Press, Bath

Contents

List of illustrations

To Cath with memories of a happy time in France

Acknowledgements

My thanks are due to the many firms who have contributed both photographs and information to help in compiling this book, also to the many fishermen who have taken me to sea and helped in other ways to give an insight into the problems of fishing boats.

Introduction

The variety of fishing boats is vast. Even restricting the selection to the smaller types, there is still a wide choice, and it is in the field of small fishing boats that many specialized types of craft have been developed to meet local conditions. Some of these craft have been developed over hundreds of years, and represent the finest seagoing craft in existence.

The choice facing the fisherman is bewildering today. Traditional craft are still built but their costs are rising because they are designed to be built by traditional methods. Some of these designs have been adapted to modern materials such as glass-reinforced plastic (GRP) and ferro-cement, whilst at the same time a new range of designs specifically suited to these new materials has emerged. In addition, there are many designs which are aimed at taking advantage of steel and aluminium construction.

Where does the fisherman go for advice when selecting a hull design for a fishing boat? If he chooses a traditional design he may miss some of the advantages which modern materials can offer. Yet he cannot really afford to experiment; when he buys a new boat it has to last for perhaps twenty years. At the same time the boat has to be adaptable to changing fishing patterns which occur all too frequently these days.

The aim of this book is firstly to look at the shape of hulls, their performance, and the materials from which they are built. The length of vessel under consideration is arbitrarily limited to around 70 feet (21 m); above this size fishing boats become ships, both in shape and construction, and the problems are different.

After hulls, the book will look at engines and the whole question of propulsion, the factors which make for reliability, so important in these days when no cost-conscious fisherman can afford to have to lay up his boat for repairs. Equally important is deck machinery and its installation because without this one cannot fish.

Electronic equipment is playing an ever-increasing role, both for navigation and for fish finding. How does a fisherman, with little training in the subject, select the best equipment for his purpose? This book will provide most of the answers, showing the alternatives and their capabilities, so that a fisherman can decide what is best for his particular purpose.

Fifty years ago there would have been no requirement for a book such as this. Fishing boats were simple, there was little choice in methods of construction and equipment was limited. Boats would be built by local boatbuilding firms and a fisherman would have little interest in developments in other parts of the country, or in other countries.

Things have changed dramatically. It is not unusual for a fisherman to have his boat built in another country and perhaps to obtain the equipment for his boat from two or three other countries. The range of choice is wide and because the equipment side, particularly, constitutes big business, the fisherman is subject to the pressures of advertising persuasion.

As equipment becomes more and more advanced, the fisherman, no matter how capable, is not always able to assess the potential of new equipment and to decide whether it will be suitable for his purpose. Economics will have a large bearing on the choice. Can a cheaper piece of equipment serve the same purpose as something more expensive for the particular application in mind?

Fishermen are having to become more and more cost conscious as the profit margins from fishing are narrowed. No longer can equipment be fitted regardless of cost; each item must be considered on its merits. Choice is not restricted to initial costs; installation can affect reliability and the way the boat is operated, so these aspects are given critical examination.

This book will be of value both to fishermen contemplating the building of a new boat and to those adding to their existing boats. More and more fishermen are building or fitting out their own boats, and much of the information contained in this book will help to guide them along the right lines.

Boats are complex pieces of equipment. The multitude of systems, mechanical, electrical, hydraulic and electronic, all present their particular difficulties. When one considers that these systems are fitted to a craft which may have to operate under severe weather conditions, one has some idea of the magnitude of the problem.

Boats can, and do, operate successfully. Faults, when they do occur, are usually the result of lack of attention to small details. The aim of this book is to examine in detail the many features of fishing boats so that all those associated with their design, construction and operation can benefit. The end product will be better fishing boats and better fishing.

CHAPTER 1

Hull Design and Construction

The hull of a fishing boat has to perform many functions. Most important, it has to keep the sea on the outside, but it also has to be the right shape to negotiate rough seas yet still be economical to drive through the water. It has to provide a platform for the fishing operations and be capable of withstanding the many stresses they impose. It has to be built to last for many years with a minimum of maintenance yet at the same time its cost has to be kept down to reasonable levels.

A fishing boat is one of the few types of craft which actually work at sea. Most vessels just carry cargoes or people so that the design factors are considerably simplified. During fishing operations there are many factors which affect the boat which are difficult to assess during the design stage, and only experience shows what is successful.

This is one of the reasons why the design of fishing boat hulls is often conservative and slow to change and yet for all the problems involved, fishermen are always prepared to experiment. Not all the experiments are successful, but gradually design progresses.

One of the first choices facing a fisherman who wants a new boat is the material to build it in. From the narrow choice of a few years ago which limited building to wood or steel, there have been added modern materials such as GRP, ferro-cement and aluminium. Each material brings its own problems both in construction and maintenance, and in most cases the material selected affects the permissible hull shapes if costs are to be kept at reasonable levels.

Wood is the traditional material for building fishing boats and the normal method of construction is to use wooden planking fastened to frames. Most hull shapes can be built fairly easily by this method, but difficulties do arise in some of the shapes around the stern where sharp curves can lead to construction problems. With wooden construction, sharp curves should generally be avoided because it is difficult to bend the wood to this shape, so wooden boats generally have gentle curves.

Wooden boats are in service all over the world and, if well constructed

Fig 1   A typical transom sterned French fishing boat built in wood.

Fig 2   An older US wooden fishing boat operating off New England. The dory on the wheelhouse roof serves as a safety boat, but would be very difficult to launch quickly in an emergency.

using good materials, they can have a life of thirty years or more. There are no short cuts to building a wooden boat, and the building of such a craft is a very labour-intensive operation which has led to rapidly increasing costs over the past few years. Add to this the difficulty in obtaining suitable quality timber in many parts of the world and it becomes obvious why fishermen have looked for other construction materials for their craft.

Many fishermen are still prepared to pay a premium for a wooden boat. It is a material which is known and understood which is an important factor when working in rough seas. A fisherman must have confidence in his boat. Repairs to wooden boats can be carried out in most parts of the world, but fewer boatyards are capable of dealing with the heavier types of wooden construction used for fishing boats.

In order to keep the costs of wooden boats down, attempts have been made to build boats from plywood panels. This has been made possible by the development of reliable grades of marine plywood, but because plywood can only be bent in one plane at a time, there are considerable restrictions on the hull shapes which can be produced. Plywood is particularly suited to boats of the hard chine type, which have large flat surfaces with only gentle curves in one plane.

A modern development of marine plywood is the building of hulls from either the cold or hot moulding process. In these methods the hull is

Fig 3   A 75 foot wooden fishing boat built by Desco in the USA. She is typical of the southern USA type of fishing boat which is finding increasing favour in northern waters largely because of the attractive price.

5

Fig 4   The Catfish 36, a catamaran fishing vessel specifically designed for beach launching
and recovery. It is powered by a diesel engine in each hull. Construction is in plywood or
aluminium.

constructed from several thin layers of wood which are laid up with the
grain running in different directions over a simple wooden former. Fairly
sharp double curves can be accommodated and the completed hull comes
out as a rigid unit which requires little additional stiffening. With this type
of hull the design is purposefully given double curves because these impart
strength to the completed hull. The type of glue used is all important and
modern cold curing glues have largely made the hot moulded process
obsolete.

Hulls built by the cold moulding process are reliable if the timber used is
selected carefully. The same applies to normal timber construction, but
here there has to be a slight over-design to allow for knots and shakes in the
timber and for eventual deterioration in the timber and fastenings. Many
authorities have produced tables of scantlings for wooden fishing boats
based on long experience with this material, and following these scales
should give a boat which is sound.

The fastenings used in wooden hulls are as important as the timber itself.
The ideal is some material which will not corrode easily, such as bronze or
stainless steel, but these are usually ruled out on cost grounds in favour of
galvanized steel. For a long life the galvanizing must be carefully done, and
it helps to preserve the fastenings if they are greased before insertion.

Often it is not the fastening itself which deteriorates, but the timber around it – the cause being electrolytic decay – the dissimilar metals of the galvanizing and (say) a bronze sea cock setting up electrical currents in the damp wood. Nevertheless, galvanized steel fastenings have proved to be a reasonable compromise between initial cost and long life, and match well with the heavy timbers used in fishing boat building.

The timbers used will vary from country to country depending on availability. Oak is available in many countries and is generally used for the main timbers such as keels and frames. These latter timbers are ideally grown to the required shape so that the grain is true, but in the interests of cost, sawn frames in two or more pieces are now commonly used. Soft wood such as pine is used for the planking, with varieties such as Oregon pine or pitch pine being most durable.

Many of the exotic African hardwoods are finding a place in boat building, with iroko, which has similar properties to teak, being one of the favourites. For moulded construction and plywood, mahogany and alternative African hardwoods are popular.

Steel is a much more consistent material than wood and has been used for boats with engines almost since marine engines have been in use. Steel

Fig 5   A 54 foot steel trawler built for use in British waters. The engine is placed well forward to give a large fish hold.

7

has much to offer now that modern welding techniques have greatly simplified boat building in this material. Despite its many advantages, steel has taken a long time to gain acceptance for building boats and it is only in recent years that it is being widely used for craft of 25 feet (8m) in length or less.

Steel can be bent to double curves, but this is expensive and requires additional skill and time. For this reason most steel hulls are built to utilize plating with a single curve which greatly simplifies construction. Indeed, steel hulls are becoming very angular as designers attempt to reduce the need to bend frames to shape as much as possible. Straight frames make for simple construction.

Steel hulls tend to depart considerably from their wooden counterparts in shape. If a single chine gives too hard a line at the bilge then a double chine is introduced, softening the hull lines but making construction easy. Steel hulls tend to incorporate large flat surfaces and these have to be adequately stiffened by internal framing to prevent distortion. As with timber hulls, long experience with steel hulls has enabled classification societies to produce tables of scantlings which, if followed, will ensure that a hull is adequately strong. These tables of scantlings detail plate thickness, frame spacing and size and cover all aspects of construction from beam knees to keel sizes.

Fig 6   The hull of the Gerryann C. under construction showing the twin chine configuration at the bilge which is simpler to construct than a rounded bilge.

Fig 7   A stern view of the Gerryann C. The ribbing reduces damage to the transom when the gear is being shot and hauled. The hull lines are fined away aft to give a good water flow to the propeller.

Repairing steel hulls is a relatively simple process and the required skills are widely available. Denting of the hull is more difficult to cope with, but in many cases there is little loss of hull strength and the dents can be left unless appearance is important. Corrosion can be a much more serious problem and the effect of this can be considerably reduced by careful attention during building and the application of special protective finishes.

Glass-reinforced plastics (GRP) are being increasingly used for fishing boat hulls. This material is made from fine glass strands which are impregnated with a polyester resin. When the resin sets after a few hours the resulting material is both tough and hard. The glass strands come in many forms, the most common being a random mat, but greater strength of laminate can be achieved by using a woven glass mat called woven rovings.

The GRP is generally laid up in a female mould by a hand lay-up process. Some builders have introduced the use of special spray equipment which combines the resin and the glass fibre, greatly simplifying the lay-up process. While the latter method produces a more consistent lay-up, the short lengths of glass strand used do not produce such a strong laminate as the hand lay-up method.

Skill and care is required in all materials used for boat building, but with GRP a much greater percentage of the strength of the finished product depends on the way in which the builders have handled the material. Defects in the construction of wooden or steel boats can usually be detected when the hull is completed, but this is rarely the case with GRP hulls. If the defects are not seen as the laminate is being laid-up, they can remain locked within the laminate until they may show their presence at a much later date.

It is for this reason that the major firms using GRP exercise very strict quality control over their hull construction. The materials which go into the hull are carefully monitored and the whole laying-up operation is overseered by inspectors. The right conditions of temperature and humidity are important in laying-up the hull and to ensure that it cures properly.

Good quality GRP construction can only be carried out in buildings constructed for this work. Many of the problems associated with early GRP hulls were caused by failure to appreciate this point and it is only by careful attention to detail that modern GRP hulls have achieved their present reliability. This costs money and the GRP hull no longer has a large price advantage over its wood and steel competitors. Price increases in the raw materials and high mould and inspection costs have largely reduced the gap.

It is for this reason that GRP fishing boat builders have turned to emphasizing the maintenance-free aspect of their hulls to encourage sales. There is no doubt that over the years the maintenance on a GRP hull will

Fig 8   A small inshore lobster boat built from foam sandwich GRP. Note how the wheel-house is recessed well into the forecastle head to make maximum use of space.

Fig 9   A 36 foot GRP hull fitted out as a combination lobster boat/trawler. The accommoda-tion is placed under the foredeck with access from the wheelhouse.

be less than on a comparable wooden or steel hull, but it is not maintenance free and will certainly require to be given an annual overhaul in the same way as wooden or steel hulls.

As with the construction of the hull, so great care has to be exercised in the fitting out of a GRP hull. Most boat builders know and appreciate the problems associated with fitting out a wooden or a steel hull, but there are many who think that a GRP hull can be treated in the same way as a wooden hull. The finished result may look good and work well, but the defects will only start to show through after several years of use. One of the main omissions is failure to seal the edges of the laminate when holes are cut in it. Water or oil finding its way into the laminate can gradually break it down.

The high cost of the mould for GRP hulls and the special conditions under which hulls have to be moulded make it logical for speciaized firms to undertake this work. This ensures the required high quality of the

Fig 10   Boats which have to dry out at moorings are best fitted with a shallow keel. The deep keel on this GRP hull allows the boat to heel over considerably even though bilge keels are fitted.

hull, but then these hulls are made available to any boatbuilder or individual who wants to undertake the fitting out. Poor standards of fitting out can spoil a high quality hull and any fisherman having a GRP hull fitted out by a firm other than the hull moulder is advised to look into this aspect carefully.

There is also the question of responsibility for the finished boat. If the hull and fitting out are done by one boat builder there is no difficulty over responsibility for the finished boat, but if the hull is built by one firm and fitted out by another, each is likely to blame the other if there are any defects on completion, with the owner in the middle trying to get his boat completed to his satisfaction.

Now that GRP has lost its image as a new wonder material and its problems are largely understood, it is gradually gaining in popularity with fishermen, particularly for the smaller sizes of boat. Tables of scantlings and methods of construction have been produced by classification societies and GRP is now a highly respected and understood material for building fishing boats.

The high cost of the GRP mould normally restricts GRP hull construction to specialized firms. A method of GRP construction which does not need an expensive mould is the GRP foam sandwich construction. This method is used for the construction of individual yachts, but is finding little favour for fishing boat construction.

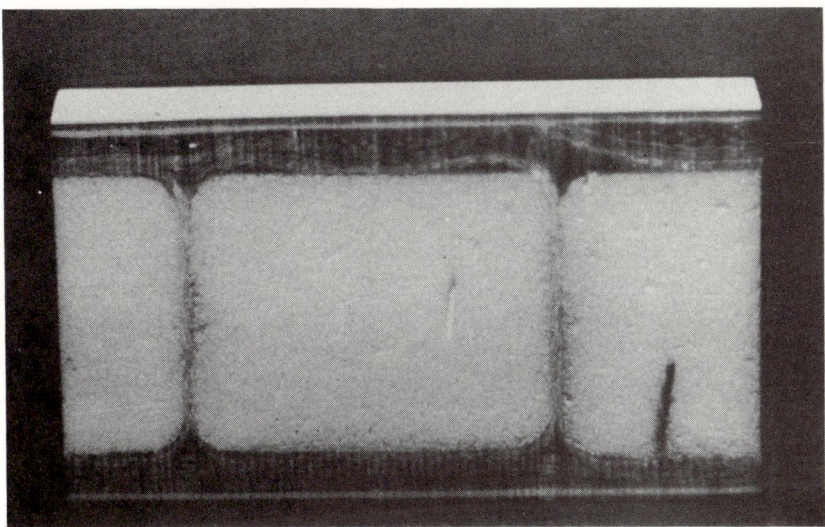

Fig 11 Foam sandwich construction showing the two layers of GRP on the outside with the foam core. This particular sample has linking members which join the two skins adding greatly to the strength and durability of the finished material.

In this method plastic foam sheeting is secured over a light timber framework to form the hull shape. A skin of GRP is laid over this foam and, when cured, the foam is lifted off the timber mould and a further GRP skin is applied to the inside of the hull. The resulting structure is very rigid and has excellent insulation and soundproofing properties. Much of the strength of the hull comes from obtaining a good bond between the GRP laminate and the foam, and great care has to be taken in fitting out to ensure that water cannot find its way into the foam through hull fastenings.

A patented method of GRP construction uses the glass strands and resin made up in the form of thin planks. These are laid over a simple frame mould and then covered with resin and mat. The simplicity of this C-flex construction has led to many fishermen using it to construct their own hulls, but boatyards also use the method when building individual designs.

A popular method of GRP construction in America uses end grain balsa wood as a core. The outer skin of the hull is laid up in a mould in the same way as in normal GRP construction, then the thin sheets of balsa, backed with a fabric, are laid over the laminate. These are impregnated with resin before an inside skin of laminate is applied. This gives a thicker hull without too much increase in weight, and because it is more rigid it requires little internal framing.

Repairs to sandwich types of hull are comparatively simple, but if water finds its way into the core through damage it is almost impossible to remove and can lead to rapid deterioration of the hull. The use of closed cell foam which does not absorb water is an improvement, but hulls of foam sandwich material remain suspect because the construction method makes it suitable for use by boat building firms who may not have suitable buildings and facilities to handle GRP satisfactorily.

The same applies to hulls constructed from ferro-cement. So many hulls built from this material are constructed in back yards in far from ideal conditions so that the quality of these hulls may be suspect. Yet ferro-cement hulls, carefully built with skilled supervision, have proved that they can stand up to hard use as fishing boats.

Ferro-cement hulls are based on a steel frame. This frame is built up from reinforcing rods which are then covered with a wire mesh. When the frame is complete, it is covered with a special cement mortar, which, when set, forms the reinforced cement hull. No additional frames or moulds are needed other than the steel reinforcing frame, but this must be strong enough to support the weight of the wet mortar before it sets. Many hulls have been ruined by sagging during the drying stage.

Generally speaking, ferro-cement hulls can be constructed to any shape to which the steel reinforcing can be shaped. Therefore there is less restriction on the hull shape, as is the case with wood and steel. Double

Fig 12   The armature of steel rods and wire mesh for a ferro–cement hull. This is now ready
for applying the cement mortar. The temporary cover gives protection from too quick
drying.

curved surfaces are preferable to single curves and flat surfaces as the
double curves impart a great deal of rigidity to the hull.

Where ferro-cement hulls are built by simply plastering on a steel
framework there is a fairly high labour factor in building the framework,
but the cost of this is offset by the cheapness of the materials. Boats can be
built in quantity this way and there are savings in mass-producing the
frames and other parts of the structure. Attempts are now being made to
produce ferro-cement hulls in quantity by the use of moulds. The steel
framework is erected inside the mould and the plastering becomes a much
simpler job when the mortar can be laid up against the hard surface of the
mould.

Using a mould in this way is likely to produce a much more consistent
result and the finish of the hull will be better. As with GRP hulls, it is very
difficult to assess the quality of a ferro-cement hull once it has been built,
and careful quality control and inspection are needed if the finished hull is
to be of an acceptable standard.

In order to simplify the construction of ferro-cement hulls, experiments are being conducted using short lengths of fine steel wire to replace the reinforcing frames and wire mesh. If these experiments are successful they will enable the mortar and reinforcing to be sprayed into the mould, considerably reducing the construction costs.

Further experiments are envisaged using glass fibre or Kevlar reinforcing for the cement mortar thus simplifying the construction further and making a stronger hull. These experiments are some way from fruition but they show that future fishermen may well be using hulls made of different materials than at present.

Ferro-cement poses problems for the boatbuilder. One of these is the difficulty in making holes for fastenings. Holes in the hull for such items as water inlets are best moulded in when the hull is constructed. This requires more thought by the hull designer than would be necessary with other materials. It is usually much more difficult to modify a ferro-cement boat, once it is built, than most other types of construction.

For all types of boats which are built in a mould, (both GRP and cement) there is a much greater freedom of choice of hull shape. The material does not restrict the shape as with wood and steel, the only restriction being on making sure that the hull will come out of the mould cleanly. For small boats a one-piece mould is used, where the hull has to be lifted out of the mould. Larger hulls often have a split mould where the two sides of the mould are taken away separately and this allows the hull to have more complex shapes if necessary.

Small GRP and ferro-cement hulls do not require internal framing, but this is generally incorporated on larger hulls to give additional stiffening so that the skin size can be kept to an economical thickness. Bulkheads also form part of the stiffening on these larger hulls and these are either moulded in or formed from marine plywood which is bonded in.

The designer of a fishing boat hull must fully understand the material from which the hull is being produced. Not only will the shape vary for different materials but methods of stiffening the hull and fastening of attachments all have to suit the material being used.

When a fisherman chooses the material from which a new boat is to be constructed, he is faced with a difficult choice. Does he choose the wooden boat which he knows but which may be expensive to build? Should he try steel, which is a tested material and can be well suited to fishing boat use if he can find a suitable yard to build it? The use of GRP or ferro-cement may be attractive because of their simplified maintenance, but hull designs which are available in these materials may be restricted. An individual design in GRP could be prohibitively expensive. Standard hulls are finding a more ready acceptance for fishing boat use, but these hulls are often designed for purposes other than fishing. In order to cover mould costs as much as possible, a GRP hull builder will try to make his hulls attractive to as wide a range of users as possible, which invariably means that some compromise has to be accepted.

The requirements of a fishing boat hull are a compromise, and each owner has to decide what his requirements are in terms of seaworthiness, speed, deck space and manoeuvrability. Only then will he be able to select the hull which is best suited to his purpose. By placing a strong emphasis on one of these aspects of hull design he may have to sacrifice some of the advantages of others.

This is particularly so where speed is concerned. The maximum speed of most fishing boats is around 9 knots, and at this speed they are operating as displacement boats. Weight is not particularly critical for this speed and weight is often added to improve the stability characteristics.

In some forms of fishing, notably shell fishing, higher speeds may be necessary to reduce time in going to and from the fishing grounds which can become more important as the distance to the grounds increases. A penalty is paid in terms of higher fuel consumption, a more expensive engine and a boat less suited to load carrying. A fisherman must look carefully at his fishing operation to see whether the higher speed is justified.

The planing boats used for high-speed work are built to a lighter form of construction because weight is critical in allowing a boat to lift in the water under the thrust from the propeller. Although lighter in weight, a planing boat is subject to higher stresses so that the hull structure is more complicated, particularly when built of wood or steel. These materials are not really suited to high-speed fishing boats and GRP is commonly used. This can provide a light rigid structure at minimum cost.

The true planing boat has a fairly large beam hull with flat underwater surfaces meeting the sides of the boat in a hard chine. Modern hull design favours the deep-V hull where the bottom sections have a deadrise up to 25°. This deadrise makes for a less efficient planing hull, but gives a much softer ride in a seaway – very desirable when working offshore. These hulls have excellent stability when underway, but it is reduced when the boat stops or is going slowly. Under these conditions the movement can be fairly lively as the initial stability is quite low, but above 10° or so of roll, the hull 'stiffens up' and the boat is quite safe at slow speeds.

Deep-V hulls can operate satisfactorily at slow speeds, but the bow usually drops at these speeds and the fine sections forward can cause water to be taken in over the bow. The same applies to the semi-displacement type of hulls which are designed for moderately high speeds, but achieve this by partly cutting through the water as well as planing on the surface. These hulls have fine sections forward with little lift which means that the bow does not lift readily to waves when proceeding at displacement speeds. Often a pronounced flare is introduced forward which rapidly improves the buoyancy once the lower fine sections have become immersed and the angle at which a wave meets the hull tends to throw water away clear.

The aft sections of these semi-displacement hulls have round bilges turning into a fairly flat bottom. The beam to length ratio is somewhere around 1:4, which reduces the working space on deck, but this is one of the penalties paid for speed. Most types of planing boat hulls terminate in a transom stern and for fishing work the wheelhouse is usually placed forward to leave a clear deck aft for working.

American fishermen have developed this type of hull into a fine seaworthy craft used mainly for potting and gill netting.

The vast majority of fishing boats are of the displacement type. Speed is rarely worth the sacrifices which have to be made to obtain it. With displacement hulls the fisherman is faced with choosing between the relative merits of seaworthiness and efficiency. This is not to say that the choice must be one or the other, but in achieving one aspect something from the other must be sacrificed in most cases. As design progresses, boats approach the ideal but this is never quite reached and a compromise must be made.

The most seaworthy type of hull is the double ender. This type has

Fig 13 A fast semi-displacement lobster boat. This vessel has a round bilge hull, but many similar vessels have a hard chine hull.

18

Fig 14   An older type of combination boat with the wheelhouse aft. In this configuration she is still rigged as a stern trawler.

evolved over centuries of use in some of the worst sea conditions in the world. A fishing boat with double pointed ends, with a deep draft, with a generous beam and freeboard and with a reliable engine is capable of riding out most storms that the sea can offer.

Not all fishing boats need these qualities. Many operate in sheltered or semi-sheltered waters where extreme sea conditions are not encountered. The boat which puts out for day fishing and returns each night is never going to be too far from shelter and so it may be able to sacrifice some of its seaworthiness qualities in order to simplify the construction or to make a better working boat.

Boats which fish more than 20 miles (32 km) from the nearest harbour should give much more attention to seaworthiness. The weather can change much in a matter of hours and by the time the change is appreciated the only course left open may be to ride out the storm. Seaworthiness is as much a matter of reliability of the hull and machinery as it is a matter of the shape of the hull, and this aspect will be discussed in later chapters.

In many parts of the world, the weather pattern is so reliable that less emphasis need be placed on seaworthiness. The effect of this is noticeable in the design of boats for these areas, where the emphasis is on a good comfortable working boat.

19

Fig 15 A specialized fishing boat designed for sheltered waters only. This oyster boat operates at Arcachon on the west coast of France and her draft allows her to operate in very shallow water. A lifting propeller and rudder are fitted to these boats.

Draft can be an important consideration in the selection of many fishing boats. Although a good deep draft of the ratio of around 1:7 of the length of the boat is desirable from the seaworthiness point of view, the depth of water available in many harbours makes a shallower draft desirable. A ratio of 1:10 is used in many modern craft and this can give much greater flexibility when entering and leaving tidal harbours.

Generally speaking the longer a boat, the greater its ability to cope with rough seas. The longer boat is less affected by the waves and is able to remain fishing long after a smaller boat has had to stop and run for shelter. This gives more fishing time with the prospect of catching more fish, but against this has to be offset the increased costs, both initial and running, of the larger boat.

The choice of the length of boat is usually dictated by the type of fishing being undertaken. For each type of fishing there is an optimum which has usually been established by a long process of trial and error. With the modern trend towards increasing legislation of fishing craft the choice of length of boat can be artificially dictated.

An example has occurred in Britain where a set of safety rules was introduced for vessels exceeding 12 metres in length. Immediately, boats were built just under this length in order to be exempt from certain aspects of the legislation and some fishermen changed to this size of craft from larger vessels. These smaller vessels were expected to fish under the same conditions as the larger craft they replaced, which demonstrates that legislation may not always have the desired effect.

In many parts of the world rules governing the licensing of craft and their crews can have a similar effect and can introduce artificial limits on design which are not always beneficial. There is a trend towards increasing the beam of small fishing craft which enables the smaller craft to perform the same work as earlier larger craft.

Increasing the beam to length ratio has been largely achieved by the introduction of the wide transom stern. By continuing the full beam sections aft there is a dramatic increase in the deck working area and a relative increase in the carrying capacity of these craft. With building and operating costs still largely related to length there has been a consequent increase in efficiency in these craft.

This break from traditional design first occurred in those craft operating in semi-sheltered sea conditions, but as designers have realized the possibilities, this trend has been extended to offshore vessels. There were forecasts that the large transom required on these vessels would result in a loss of seaworthiness and a considerable increase in power would be necessary.

There has, however, been little loss in seaworthiness and any increased tendency to broaching in a following sea has largely been counteracted by improvements to the effectiveness of steering systems. More powerful engines are generally fitted to these wide beamed boats, but this is because of a desire to have sufficient power to pull a heavier trawl to match the increased capability of these vessels rather than because the hulls are harder to drive through the water.

Having the main volume of the hull aft on these transom boats tends to give them a 'bow-down' appearance. Ballast tanks aft are often fitted to keep the stern down when running light and these are pumped out as the fish hold is filled, maintaining a fairly even trim at all times.

Stability is a much discussed problem in regard to fishing vessels and lack of it has been the cause of many losses. Fishing boats are one of the few types of craft which actually load at sea and it is extremely difficult to assess the varying stability of a hull under fishing conditions. As the stability can be increased at will to any desired level during the design stage within certain limits, it could be argued that a vessel should be made as stable as possible. The problem is that increasing the stability generally increases the violence of the motion of the vessel. A fishing vessel has to be able to work at sea and this cannot be done if the motion is too violent, so a compromise has to be reached between adequate stability and a comfortable motion.

With fuel and ice being used up and the catch being loaded the stability criteria are changing constantly. The wave patterns are also changing continuously and there are certain wave patterns which are detrimental to stability. Synchronous rolling can occur when the natural period of roll of the hull matches that of the waves passing it. This normally results in only one or two heavier rolls because the wave frequency changes rapidly, but if it continues it can result in capsize if the heading is not altered.

When a vessel is running before a following sea, an equal danger to broaching is the loss of stability when the vessel becomes poised for some time on the crest of a wave. Under these conditions the stability can be halved and if the sea is shipped at the same time, disaster may be imminent. The trend towards wide beamed hulls has done much to improve stability characteristics. Previously it was thought that adding fixed ballast was the answer.

Fixed ballast may be used to improve the trim of a boat but as a means of improving stability it can be self-defeating unless it is carefully distributed through the hull. Adding ballast may improve the initial stability, but it also reduces the freeboard which is an important factor in maintaining the range of stability. The stability shows a dramatic reduction once the deck edge becomes immersed.

The distribution of fixed ballast can affect the motion of the hull, and rather than fix it all as low as possible in the bilge it can help to spread it out into the bilges. Not only will this improve the motion of the hull, but it will also avoid heavy concentrations of weight which can put high stresses on the hull structure. Concrete is a popular ballast material on steel and wooden boats, often encasing scrap iron to increase the weight concentration. On GRP boats, steel punchings are used encapsulated in resin.

The line of the deck sheer can be an important factor in fishing vessel design. A pronounced sheer can help to maintain stability while at the same time keeping the freeboard reasonably low in the working areas. The high bow and stern also help to keep the decks dry when operating in head or following seas and give plenty of reserve buoyancy to the forward sections to help them to ride over waves. Deck sheer is largely absent from fast boat designs because the change in trim as the bow lifts would reduce visibility from the wheelhouse unless the deck had a level or reverse sheer. This is one of the main reasons why these craft are less suited to working offshore.

Among all these conflicting requirements, the fisherman somehow has to choose a hull design for a new boat. He will have some idea of his requirements based on his previous fishing experience and what he expects of the new boat. With the pattern of fishing changing in many areas of the world there is a trend away from specialized craft to more general purpose types which can be speedily adapted to be suitable for whatever type of fishing is profitable.

A fisherman may adopt a conservative approach and choose a type which is already operating successfully in his home port, perhaps introducing a few ideas of his own. This is how fishing boats have evolved over the years, producing characteristic designs which are used in a particular locality. From experience these craft have been found to match the operating conditions at that locality. This is particularly so for boats launched from open beaches.

With fishermen becoming less insular there is a marked trend to look outside the narrow confines of a particular locality to see what other fishermen are doing. There is now a much greater interchange of ideas amongst fishermen, largely sponsored by the fishing press, and this is the situation which the builders of standard boats, mainly steel and GRP, hope to exploit. They find or produce a successful design and series production enables them to offer this at a very competitive price.

The success of this method depends a great deal on the design used, but an example is that of one Cornish firm who have carefully adapted a traditional hull design to GRP production. This is selling to several countries in Europe as well as to widely diverse fishing areas in Great Britain. This leads one to the conclusion that hull design is not as specific to particular localities as many fishermen imagine, and a good design can be successful under a wide variety of conditions.

If a fisherman favours an existing type of boat then it is advisable to go to sea in one already in use. This will provide assurances as to the capabilities of the particular hull selected, and also show how that particular boat works. This will enable him to discuss the siting of the various components on the boat with the boat builder more knowledgeably.

Eventually, the fisherman himself is responsible for the finished boat. It is no good blaming the boatyard if something is wrong or has not been fitted in the right place. The fisherman should have explained exactly what he wanted and then made sure it was done. Most traditional builders of fishing boats have a good knowledge of what fishermen require and will produce a boat which will work, but there are many boatyards who do not have this ability.

A successful fishing boat requires a great deal of planning and thought. The naval architect should be able to translate a fisherman's ideas into a working boat and supervise its construction, but he is unlikely to have the deep knowledge of fishing which is required to ensure that the finished product is a good fishing boat. Too many fishermen treat the building of a new boat in a casual manner. For something which probably has to be the basis of a livelihood for the next thirty years, it deserves a better start.

CHAPTER 2

Engines

This book will consider engines ranging from simple hand-start inboard engines and outboard motors to large diesel engines of up to 500 hp. Whatever their size careful attention to both their installation and maintenance is necessary if they are to be reliable. Reliability is all important in a fishing boat, not only from the point of view of safety but because a boat whose engine is not operating cannot earn money.

Fishermen in general take many chances with their engines. Even though the initial installation may be sound, poor maintenance can soon reduce the reliability, and often a defect is not detected or is ignored until the engine stops at sea or will not start when it is time to set off for sea. An engine failure at sea can quickly put a vessel in danger. At best, it means a tow back into harbour and time wasted while repairs are carried out. It would have been much better to have planned time into the fishing programme to carry out preventative maintenance.

A fishing boat is only earning money when it is at sea fishing. Generally fishing boats only have one engine. With two engines it would be possible for the boat to continue fishing even if one were out of action for repairs. There are arguments against two engines: the initial cost is higher and with twin screws the propellers are more vulnerable. This latter point can be covered by having a main engine and a wing engine away from the working side. Cost must be weighed against the importance of keeping the boat fishing. If two engines are fitted then it is important to keep the systems for each engine as separate as possible so that a defect on one will not affect the other.

Any engine installation starts with the engine beds. Unless the engine has a firm base there will be problems with vibration and alignment which will give continual trouble. The engine beds, whatever material the hull is constructed from, should extend for at least twice the length of the engine and gearbox, so as to spread the load adequately. It is the engine beds which transmit the thrust from the propeller throughout the hull structure.

Fig 16   The engine beds on this GRP hull can be clearly seen. They help to spread the engine load throughout the hull. The battery stowage on the top right is good.

The engine beds should be capable of supporting not only the weight of the engine, but also the greatly increased stresses which can occur when the boat moves in a seaway. On a high speed boat these stresses can be several times the weight of the engine as the boat rises and falls rapidly in waves. In wooden and GRP hulls the engine beds are usually topped with a steel angle section which helps to spread the high local loadings from the engine feet.

Most fishing boat engines are solidly mounted onto the engine beds which considerably simplifies the engine installation, because no allowance has to be made in the connecting piping for the slight engine movements. A good installation with solid beds will prevent undue vibration, but where vibration is excessive, flexible mounts are sometimes used.

The type of engine selected will have a bearing on the selection of mountings. A single cylinder diesel may have considerable vibration whereas a four cylinder petrol engine would be much smoother. Six cylinder in-line engines are generally smoother and V-six and V-eight engines are better still. Smooth running will be only one of the factors which will affect the choice of engine and is likely to be low on the list of priorities.

Fig 17 A six cylinder Gardner diesel mounted on massive steel engine beds in a wooden hulled fishing boat. Note the steel bulkhead for the engine compartment which is fitted to meet fire regulations.

The choice of engine must be related to what is available. There may be a considerable waiting list for some of the better engines and unless a delay is acceptable these should be ruled out. The choice between petrol and diesel engines will be largely decided by local fuel supplies. Petrol engines are generally cheaper than a similar power, of diesel engine, but their fuel consumption will be higher and the fuel is usually more expensive. There may be weight advantages with high speed boats, in using a petrol engine, but even this advantage is being negated as lighter powerful diesels become available.

The diesel engine is proving to be the most popular for fishing boats. Diesel fuel, with its higher flash point, is much safer than petrol, where great care has to be taken over the installation of the fuel system. Petrol is mostly used on outboard engines and these are still in use on many small open fishing boats. Their advantage is simple installation, and an engine which can be quickly removed from the boat both for servicing and security.

The power required from an engine to obtain a given speed can be calculated by naval architects. Marine engine builders will often supply the same information gleaned from experience with a great variety of hull shapes and engine installations. If the vessel is to be used for trawling, additional power will be required to pull the trawl. In specialized trawling craft there is a tendency to fit excessively powerful engines so that the boat can pull a large trawl. There can be some advantage in such engines for other fishing purposes.

If the engine fitted to a fishing boat is just powerful enough to propel the boat at the required speed when running at maximum revolutions per minute (rpm), it will in all probability show a higher fuel consumption than a larger engine producing the same power at lower rpm. The larger engine can be run at speeds in the region where it produces optimum torque and so is at its most efficient. Running at higher rpm, while quite feasible, does not produce an increase in power in proportion to the increase in r.p.m.

With fuel costs continually rising any saving in fuel consumption should be considered, but this must be offset against the higher initial cost of a larger engine and its installation. It is generally worthwhile to fit the larger engine because it offers other benefits as well. When working in a head sea, the resistance of the hull can be increased by a third or more and the reserve of power will enable the boat to maintain speed. There will also be a margin for towing a trawl. Even though this may not have been considered in the original design, a change in the pattern of fishing may force a change in tactics and make trawling desirable.

A reserve of power can also compensate for marine growth on the hull giving added hull resistance, although the best remedy is to clean the hull because fuel is being wasted. Finally, a reserve of power will allow a sufficient margin to drive additional auxiliaries from the engine should this become necessary.

After the horsepower which will give the required reserve has been decided, the choice is then whether to have a lighter high revving diesel or a slower revving heavy diesel. The initial cost of the high revving diesel is likely to be less, but over the years it will probably show greater wear and require more frequent maintenance and overhaul.

There is a marked preference for the heavy slower revving diesel among fishermen because the high inertia of the moving parts of the engine means that the engine will maintain a steady speed even though the loading on the propeller is varying owing to changing sea conditions. This moderates the effect of waves on the hull and keeps the boat running evenly. The same effect could be achieved on the high revving diesel by fitting a large flywheel, but because these engines are often converted truck engines this is not practicable. It is advisable to select an engine which has been designed specifically as a marine engine rather than a truck engine which has been converted for marine use, but because of quantity production the cost of the converted engine is usually lower, and economic factors can influence the choice.

Because of the need to reduce, as far as possible, the time during which a fishing boat engine is under repair or overhaul, it is important to consider the service facilities existing locally for the engine. Spare parts must be readily available and this, more than any other factor, is likely to govern the choice of engine. The possibility of a change in fishing base means that engine manufacturers having widespread service facilities must be considered. This is where the converted truck engines may prove to be a better choice. With a much wider market manufacturers of such engines can generally offer better service facilities.

Fig 18   A diesel engine fitted in a small fishing boat. Access for maintenance is not easy with this layout but it gives short runs for the hydraulic piping to the winch.

Accessibility has to be considered both in the selection of the engine and in the design of the boat. If an engine is to receive the attention it deserves it is vital that the parts which have to be serviced are easy to reach. The more overhaul work which can be done with the engine in its mounting, the cheaper will be the general maintenance costs and the less time involved. For example, consider the big-end bearings. If the design of both the engine bearers and the crankcase and sump allows for these to be replaced without removal of the engine, then the time involved in renewing bearings will be much less than if the engine has to be removed from the boat.

Arrangements should always be made in the design of the hull and superstructure for the engine and gearbox to be removed from the boat without undue dismantling of the hull. It is not always possible to arrange for a direct opening through the deck as the deck space may be required for winches or fish hold access. It is common to find the engine placed under the wheelhouse or superstructure. Hatches in the deck corresponding to a bolted on wheelhouse top can give the required access, but this has to be carefully planned if it is to be successful.

Some fishing boat builders arrange engine installation to suit their own convenience. It is much easier to install the engine into the hull of a new boat before the deck is fitted. Many parts of the boat's structure are then built around the engine and the problems thus caused may only come to light years later when the engine has to be taken out. If the engine is put in after the deck and superstructure have been fitted to the hull, most of the important parts of the engine will have to be accessible to allow the engine to be connected up.

There must be adequate space around the engine for access to the various parts which require maintenance and these parts must be equally accessible when at sea. If it is easy to look around the engine compartment when at sea, small defects can often be detected before they cause a complete engine failure or worse. One point so often overlooked in fishing boat design is access to the engine compartment. Lifting heavy hatches at sea with the boat tossing about can be both difficult and dangerous.

Hinged hatches are much easier to handle and there should be some means of securing them in an open position. Ideally, access to the engine should be from inside the superstructure, but if this is not possible, as is often the case in smaller boats, then the hatches should protect the opening from the sea and spray as far as possible when open. This can be achieved by dividing the hatch and hinging it on the outboard side.

Easy access to the engine compartment encourages regular inspection. An alternative to opening the hatches is to fit a transparent insert into the hatches or a bulk-head. This, combined with putting the switch for the engine compartment lights outside the compartment, will enable the engines to be seen and checked without going down below. It is not as good as a close examination but it is better than none at all.

The engine compartment must be fitted with handholds. Hot exhausts and moving driving belts can make it dangerous down below if there is nothing to hold on to when the boat is rolling. If all the important components such as sea cocks, piping, filters *etc* are made accessible it then becomes a simple matter to check the systems for leakage and defects.

On many boats, particularly larger craft, it is common practice to fit much of the piping under steel floorplates. Being out of sight leads to neglect. The first sign of trouble is often water rising above the floor plates. Any plates fitted should be easy to lift and preferably made from non-skid material. This latter quality is not easy to achieve with spilt oil about, and chequered aluminium plate is a good compromise.

One reason for making the engine compartment as large as possible is that it helps to dissipate the heat from the engines. Engine compartments can become very hot, particularly just after the engine has been stopped and the engine inspired air circulation has stopped. This can be harmful to the electrical installation, and if ventilation fans are fitted these should be left on for a few minutes to help cool the compartment.

Engines require large quantities of air if they are to keep running and that arriving at the air intake should be as cool as possible for maximum efficiency. The air from outside should be ducted to the lower part of the engine compartment so that hot air in the compartment is forced up and out through the exhaust vents. The positioning of the air intake on deck requires careful thought if it is to work satisfactorily. Two obvious requirements are that the air is kept well away from the exhaust so that

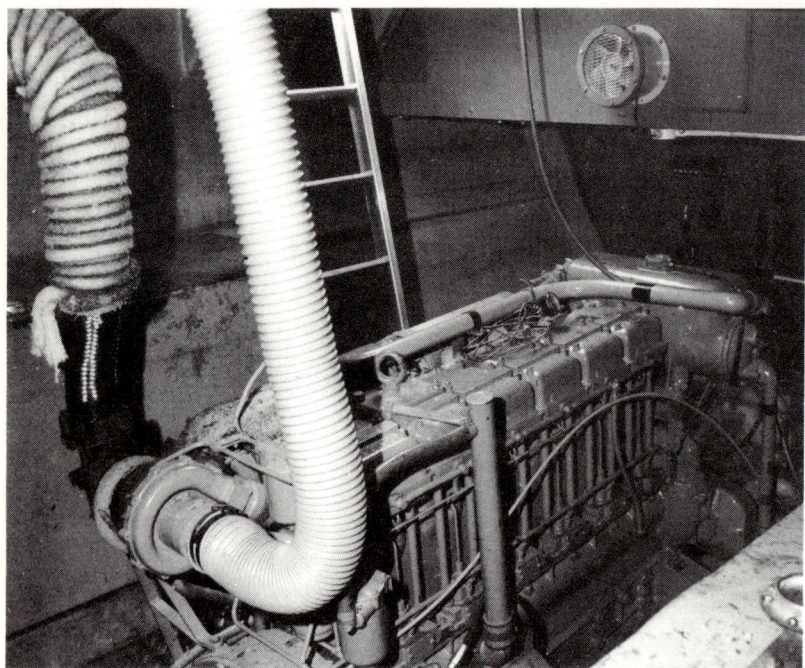

Fig 19   An air-cooled six cylinder diesel. The fan above the engine helps to give good ventilation in the engine compartment. Note the separate duct to take the air supply to the engine air intake.

Fig 20   The engine air intake below the outside wheel is placed too close to the deck and salt
water could enter.

fumes are not recirculated and that water cannot easily get into the engine
compartment. The first requirement is easy to achieve, but the second is
often given little consideration on many smaller boats. In many cases, one
sees a simple grill fitted near deck level, often in the engine hatch itself, so
that any water on deck will quickly find its way down below. The quantity
involved is usually small and it can be readily pumped out, but being salt, it
is very corrosive and can lead to rapid deterioration of fittings in the engine
components, particularly the electrical units.

The air inducted to cool the engines can be made to perform other
functions as well. One of the main causes of hull deterioration both on
wooden and steel vessels, and to a certain extent on GRP vessels, is pockets
of damp stale air being retained in the hull structure. These lead to rot and
corrosion but with careful planning and ducting it should be possible to
arrange for the engine air to be drawn through the hull, keeping the
structure sweet and dry.

Drawing the air in thus will mean that the air flow to the engine will be
restricted, which will mean a slight loss of efficiency. The air passages

Fig 21   The well of a small steel vessel showing the transverse and longitudinal framing. The air intake for the air–cooled engine can be clearly seen and provision must be made in the engine cover for this.

should be made as easy as possible. Care must be taken to ensure that the air flow will not be stopped when the hull is battened down.

On boats with larger engines, electrically driven ventilation fans are often fitted to maintain a good air flow in the engine compartment. With these it is easy to arrange a good air flow through the hull and the increased hull life would justify the extra cost. To provide the air which the engine uses, two inlet fans are usually fitted, and one exhaust fan. The cool inlet air should come in at the bottom of the engine compartment and the heated exhaust air taken out at the top.

On craft with petrol engines, this air flow will help to remove dangerous fumes, but as these are heavier than air, the exhaust fan should be ducted to the bottom of the engine compartment where it will suck the fumes out. The fan motor must be spark proof so that it does not ignite the gas, and the switch should be outside the compartment. It is good practice to switch on this fan for a few minutes before starting the engine to remove any accumulated gases.

Ventilation of engine compartments is much neglected on most craft. Some thought, particularly at the design stage, would enable improvements to be made without much expense. It becomes increasingly important where air-cooled engines are used, and it is surprising that more fishermen do not take advantage of the much simpler installations which are possible with these engines.

With an air-cooled engine the flow of air to the engine compartment is vital for keeping the engine cool. It is drawn in by means of an engine-driven fan and there is no reason why it should not be drawn in around the hull as previously suggested. In fact, air drawn in in this way is likely to be cool. It is important with an air-cooled engine that the warmed exhaust air is not recirculated through the engine; it should be ducted directly outside the compartment. There is no need to duct both inlet and exhaust cooling air, but if the cooling air is drawn directly from the engine compartment it may be better to provide a direct air supply to the engine manifold inlet to ensure a good supply.

Air-cooled engines are sometimes condemned as being noisy, but this is not the case with a good installation. Apart from avoiding the complications of a water cooling system, they also provide a supply of warm air which can be ducted for heating of the vessel.

Water cooling is still the favoured means of cooling marine engines, but if the cooling system is to work satisfactorily and be safe it must be carefully planned and installed, and it does require maintenance. The pipes carrying the sea water are directly open to the sea and any leak will admit water to the engine compartment. If the leak is not detected and stemmed, the boat will start to sink.

There are three types of water cooling systems. There are some where raw sea water is circulated directly through the engine. In others the sea water is circulated through a heat exchanger where fresh water circulating around the engine is cooled. The third system uses a closed fresh water flow which is cooled by pumping the fresh water through ducts or tubes on the outside of the hull. The sea water flowing past the hull acts as the cooling agent.

The system in general use is the second, where circulated sea water cools fresh water. The system is complicated in as much as there are two separate water circuits, but it has the advantage that the engine can run at a controlled temperature, and corrosion is greatly reduced. This system became popular when truck engines were converted for marine use. Many of the components of these truck engines were not suitable for use with sea water, and the closed fresh water circuit simplified the conversion.

The engine is supplied complete with the fresh water system fitted. A header tank, usually fitted at the forward end of the engine, acts to keep the system full and usually incorporates the heat exchanger. Little maintenance is required on the fresh water side except to check for leaks and to ensure that the water pump drive belt is properly tensioned. Anti-freeze must be added in the winter in cold climates to prevent freezing.

A separate water pump, usually belt driven, maintains the flow in the sea water system. This system is subject to the same pressures as the outside of the hull and these can be quite high in the case of a high speed craft. Each sea water circuit is made specifically for the individual boat and must be carefully designed and fitted.

The water enters through a sea cock and filter. The sea cock is a valve which can be used to isolate the system either when the boat is left unattended, or in an emergency if a leak develops. A leak in the sea water cooling system will start to flood the bottom of the engine compartment and as the sea cock is invariably located in this area, often under the floor plates, it will be appreciated that it can be difficult to locate and turn off the valve in an emergency.

A safety measure is to have the spindle of the sea cock extended up to deck level so that it can be operated whatever the conditions in the engine compartment. This does not mean that the rest of the system can be ignored. While great care is taken to ensure that the hull is strong and watertight, many fishermen overlook the fact that a leak in the sea water cooling system can be just as bad as a hole in the hull.

The piping of the cooling system should be rigid as far as practicable, but it may be necessary to introduce short lengths of flexible pipe to reduce vibration. These lengths of flexible pipe must be of the reinforced type, preferably of neoprene rubber, which stands up well to sea water. They must be secured to the rigid piping by means of double stainless steel clips. Any other type will corrode rapidly. All the piping must be secured against movement and it is good practice to renew the piping every few years as a precaution against internal corrosion. The lengths of flexible pipe should be renewed annually because they give little warning of failure.

The same standards should be followed throughout the system and if the pipes are located where they can be easily seen there is a chance of a defect being noted before it becomes serious. Warning of a leak or a stoppage in the flow can be obtained by fitting a flow meter in the system. This will indicate if the flow stops and can be connected to an alarm bell. Positioning of such a meter in the system needs to be carefully thought out. If placed close to the sea cock it will still register a flow even if the system is leaking. Probably the best position is in the pipe leading away from the heat exchanger. It will then give an indication if the pump itself fails for any reason.

It is normal to fit a temperature gauge and alarm into the fresh water side of the circuit. This will certainly indicate if the engine is overheating, but the whole fresh water system must heat up before it will do so, and meanwhile a great deal of water could have entered the hull through a defect in the seawater system.

With sea water cooling throughout the engine, the temperature gauge will indicate any fault in the system fairly quickly. Corrosion can be a major problem on this type of installation particularly if dissimilar metals are present. A brass water pump and steel cylinder head will set up electrolytic action which will be increased if galvanized piping is used. Sacrificial anodes can be fitted in the cooling system similar to those fitted to the outside of the hull and these will reduce the wastage of vital parts of the engine.

Raw sea water cooling is currently generally restricted to the smaller one or two cylinder diesel engines. It is also used on several types of petrol engine and offers the benefit of simplicity, but is likely to lead to a reduced engine life.

The use of keel tubes for cooling the fresh water in a totally enclosed system would appear to offer several advantages over the other two cooling systems. With no sea water circulating inside the hull it is safer and the installation inside the hull is less complicated. The main disadvantages are the vulnerability of the tubes outside the hull, particularly from damage by fishing gear and warps, and the difficulty in repairing any leak. Such repairs entail slipping the boat. A leak is unlikely to disable the boat completely as the contaminated water would still circulate.

It seems that the use of keel cooling systems will increase in the future as improved cooling systems are developed. One such system has the tubes fitted as stringers inside the hull on a steel vessel. The outside skin of the hull acts as the cooling surface and the tubes act as hull stiffeners. The

Fig 22 The keel cooling ducts can be seen on this unusal photo of a steel fishing boat. They are placed close to each side of the keel to reduce the risk of damage.

problem here is the large area required for efficient cooling and the difficulty in ensuring that it is all completely watertight.

One of the main factors acting against the use of keel cooling is that engine manufacturers do not generally recommend it. These manufacturers are blamed for all sorts of defects which occur to marine engines, even though many of the factors are outside their control and in the hands of the boat builder. They would normally have little say in how a keel cooling system was installed and tend to recommend the combined fresh and sea water system because they supply the majority of the components already installed on the engine. In this regard it is worth noting that the heat exchanger may be the bare minimum required to transfer the heat. Small diameter tubes can be prone to blockage and may be difficult or impossible to clean.

The fitting of a separate large heat exchanger should be considered, but any modifications such as this should be done in co-operation with the engine manufacturer. They are normally only too pleased to help and have experts in marine engines for the purpose. Listen to these experts but remember that their prime interest is to ensure the best working conditions for their engines. They are not particularly concerned with the boat as a whole, whereas the fisherman's interest is to get a boat which will be safe, reliable and efficient at catching fish.

On many engines an additional heat exchanger is fitted into the cooling system in order to cool the engine lubricating oil. There may even be a third heat exchanger for the gearbox oil. The lubricating oil acts as an engine coolant as well as a lubricant and can only carry out these functions efficiently if it is cool. Sometimes the sump is finned to aid cooling, but this is usually a fitting on engines which were originally designed for trucks.

The lubricating oil can only keep cool if there is a sufficient quantity circulating so it is important to keep the sump topped up. It should become a habit to check the oil level before each trip to sea, but as an added check it is possible to fit an electric warning device which will indicate a low level when under way. A low level may also be indicated by a reduction in oil pressure or an increase in temperature and these gauges should be fitted together with sound alarms, as a fisherman will not always be watching the gauges when trouble arises.

Spare lubricating oil should always be carried when at sea. If carried in cans these should have a proper stowage provided. The engine compartment is no place to have loose equipment. A better system is to have a fitted tank for lubricating oil and, to simplify topping up while under way, this can be connected directly by pipe to the engine oil filler. Additional oil is added to the engine by simply opening a valve. A sight gauge on the tank can quickly indicate the quantity being added.

A similar system is employed when the engine has a dry sump. The lubricating oil pump then has two parts, one on the pressure side which directs the oil around the engine bearings, and the other a scavenge pump to clear the oil which drains to the sump and return it to the oil reservoir. This system has the advantage of a larger oil capacity, and allows the engine to be more compact, making installation easier. The use of dry sump engines is decreasing. Most marine engines today are derived from truck engines which have a wet sump system. With the wet sump system a small hand pump has to be provided to allow the sump oil to be pumped out when oil changing. It cannot be drained off in the normal manner.

The oil system is vital to the running and long life of the engine. With the self-contained systems on modern engines there should not be any problems provided the oil is changed regularly and the level maintained. Cleanliness is essential: the filters in the system will cope with a certain amount of contamination, but contamination should be avoided. In planning the engine installation it is preferable to ensure that the filters are easily accessible and that there is space to change them.

The engine exhaust system also has to be carefully planned during the installation stage if it is to operate in a trouble free manner. The object of the system is to take the engine exhaust gases away from the boat, cooling them and reducing combustion noise. There are two main types of systems, the wet exhaust and the dry exhaust.

With the wet exhaust, the exhaust manifold has a water jacket as part of the sea water circuit and the cooled gases are led into a metal or special rubber exhaust pipe into which the expelled sea water flowing from the engine is injected. This water injection both further cools the exhaust gases and provides a degree of silencing.

The exhaust pipe from the exhaust manifold is led upwards into an inverted U-bend beyond the top of which the water is injected so that it will not run back into the engine. The exhaust pipe is terminated either through the side of the boat or through the transom and the water/steam flow gives an indication that the system is functioning correctly.

Because of its flexibility, rubber exhaust piping is easy to install, it only needs securing at intervals to prevent any movement. This is leading to increasing use of this type of exhaust. While the flow of cooling water is maintained it works perfectly satisfactorily and the only maintenance required is an examination periodically to check for wear and leaks.

The main drawback with this type of exhaust is what happens if the cooling water flow stops, either through a blockage or a water pump failure. It might even be something simple like the drive belt to the pump slipping or breaking. With no cooling water the hot exhaust gases impinge directly onto the rubber and will very quickly melt and set fire to it. With a fresh water cooling system there will be no immediate warning from the temperature gauge or the alarm, and this is another case where a flow meter in the sea water system will be the only way of obtaining immediate warning of the situation.

The dry exhaust system produces no such problems, but it does require careful installation in the first place. Because the exhaust pipe is carrying hot gases the boat's structure has to be protected from the pipe. This can be done by simply lagging the pipe with asbestos, which must be maintained in good condition, or by leaving an air space around the pipe. It is particularly important to lag the exhaust pipe carefully in the engine compartment, both to protect crew moving about in this area and to reduce the fire risk if there is a fuel leak.

With the dry exhaust system it is usual to incorporate a silencer in the system which can require considerable space. Both this and the pipe should be protected from salt spray which will cause rapid corrosion of the hot metal. The flow of hot gases up the exhaust pipe can be used to induce a flow of air through a funnel or exhaust stack which in turn can be used to increase the engine room ventilation.

Fig 23   A diesel powered outdrive unit which makes a convenient installation for a small vessel. The whole unit is virtually self-contained and only requires a hole in the transom for mounting.

While all these engine systems have been described for a single engine they are equally applicable to twin engined installations. In this case the systems for each engine should be kept as separate as possible so that a fault on one engine will not put the other engine out of action. With the systems described this is not too difficult, but complications can arise with the fuel and electrical systems. Because of their importance, these systems are the subject of separate chapters, together with the auxiliary machinery which is often driven by the main engine.

Outboard motors are used on many small fishing boats. Because all the engine systems including the transmission are incorporated in one unit, they are generally very reliable, as they have been thoroughly tested. Even the separate fuel tanks and piping are purpose designed for their job. Out board motors tend to be susceptible to corrosion, and should be sprayed with a water repellent grease after each use. Regular servicing is essential and, given this, these units can give very reliable service.

Smaller outboards up to about 20 hp are simply clamped to the transom. Larger units, available up to 200 hp, are bolted onto the transom. Outboards are generally two stroke engines having a fairly high fuel consumption for the power they produce. Some four stroke outboards are produced and low horse power diesel and paraffin engines are available.

Every care must be taken with the engine installation both in terms of materials and workmanship. A casual approach will lead to trouble, which may only stop fishing, but could endanger life.

CHAPTER 3

The Fuel System

The purpose of the fuel system is to supply clean fuel to the engine in the required quantity. In practice many problems are encountered between the supply hose from the oil depot and the burning of the fuel in the combustion chambers of the engine. If petrol is the chosen fuel then the problems become more acute owing to the highly inflammable nature of the fuel. Precautions have also to be taken with diesel fuel, because, in certain conditions, it can be equally dangerous.

The fuel has to be contained in tanks on board. It is preferable to divide the fuel storage into two or more parts. If the fuel in one tank becomes contaminated with water or dirt, then the supply can always be drawn from the other tank. It is usually easier to find space in the hull for two smaller tanks rather than one large tank, and the stresses due to fuel surge are less on the smaller tank. Finally, a leak in one tank will not completely exhaust the fuel supply.

Tanks can be made from a variety of metals: steel, aluminium, copper, brass and plastic materials such as GRP. For petrol storage any of the metals are suitable, but corrosion can arise inside a steel tank which can lead to rust particles entering the system. GRP is not suitable for petrol storage but is a suitable material in which to store diesel fuel, provided that great care is taken over building the tank. The inside of the tank must have a complete covering of resin to prevent the fuel entering the laminate.

Steel can be used for constructing diesel fuel tanks, but it suffers from internal corrosion and diesel fuel is more corrosive than petrol. It is becoming a practice to coat the inside of steel fuel tanks with epoxy resin to reduce this corrosion, but the coating must be done very carefully to avoid leaving any gaps.

On small boats there is usually no access to the inside of the fuel tank once it has been constructed, but on larger craft with bigger tanks a manhole is fitted to the tank to give access for cleaning. This should only be necessary once every few years and great care must be taken that the tank is free of gas before anyone enters. An empty fuel tank, whether diesel or petrol, can contain explosive mixtures of gases so great care must be taken not to cause sparks.

Baffles are fitted to the inside of the tank to prevent the fuel surging to and fro when the boat rolls at sea. This surge can subject the tank to very high stresses, as well as having a detrimental effect on the stability of the vessel, if the tank is large. The baffles should be around four fifths of the cross sectional area of the tank and should be fitted both longitudinally and athwartships if the dimensions of the tank warrant it. On steel tanks the baffles are usually welded steel plates, and on GRP tanks they are moulded in panels of GRP. These baffles also serve to stiffen the tank.

Securing the fuel tank in the boat must be done very carefully to prevent any movement. When full, a fuel tank is heavy and this weight may be effectively doubled or trebled due to violent movement of the boat. Not only must the weight of the tank be supported, but it must be prevented from movement in any direction, even upwards!

The slightest movement of the fuel tanks will gradually increase, and there is the possibility of the movement wearing away the tank, resulting in a leak. Any movement of the tank is likely to strain the connecting pipes as well.

One of the most effective ways of securing a fuel tank is to build it in as part of the vessel's structure. This is common practice with steel boats, and is also being done on GRP craft. There is no chance of the tank moving, but there are other disadvantages. A part of the built-in tank will most likely form part of the outside plating of the hull, which can be easily damaged either by collision or by mishandling of the fishing gear. The result may be only a slight outward seepage of fuel, but it could also result in water entering the fuel. Integral tanks can also make repairs difficult, particularly on GRP boats.

Sometimes fuel is carried in double bottom tanks where the tank is less liable to damage except in the event of grounding. The disadvantage of this type of tank is that it is not possible to fit a water and sludge trap at the lowest part of the tank and more frequent cleaning would be required. Tanks built in situ are more prone to internal condensation owing to the cold outside surface of the hull.

On wooden boats, steel tanks are commonplace. They are usually shaped to fit up against the frames on the side of the boat and thus make this area of the ship's side inaccessible. This is often one of the first places where rot starts. The damp conditions can also lead to heavy corrosion of the steel of the tank. If possible, tanks on wooden boats should be fitted where there is a good circulation of air around them.

A sediment sump should be fitted at the lowest point of each tank so that any dirt and water in the fuel will settle out when the boat is at rest. The water can be drawn off at intervals, but the sediment cannot be removed until the tank is cleaned out. The purpose of the sump is to encourage the sediment to settle at the lowest point where it will not be drawn into the engine, although the movement of the boat in the sea will inevitably stir it up to a certain extent.

The filler pipe to the fuel tank leads up to the deck, where it will have an opening with a watertight screwed cover. The location of the filler on the deck requires careful thought. It needs to be readily accessible and placed where any fuel spillage will run overboard and not into the boat. The filler should be raised above the deck so that water will not lie on it, but it should be clear of the working areas where it might be damaged.

The shorter the filling pipe between the deck and the tank, the better. The pipe may be solid, but it is common practice to insert a flexible section. This must be a suitable fuel resistant pipe and be well secured with double worm drive clips. This pipe must be checked regularly or the bilges may be filled with precious fuel.

The fuel filler must be of adequate size. Although a regular fuelling station may have a small nozzle, refuelling may have to be done at a station having only a large nozzle. There is less chance of spillage with a large filler. The filler should be labelled with the type of fuel which is to be put into it to avoid mistakes.

When fuel enters or leaves the tank, air has to take its place. The vent pipe should be fitted to the highest part of the tank and close to the point where the filler enters the tank. If it is placed on the opposite side there could be a chance of fuel coming out of the vent if the tank is filled when the vessel has a list. The vent should be led above the deck to a level above the filler, where it is terminated in a gooseneck with the opening covered by fine gauze.

The vent pipe must be carefully sited so that water, either from spray or from deck washing, will not find its way down the pipe. Because fumes may come out of the pipe it should not be near accommodation or the galley and the fumes should be free to disperse rapidly.

Once completed, the fuel tank should be hydraulically tested to a pressure of 5 lb/sq in. This is normally done before the tank is installed, but it is advisable to test the whole system to this pressure after installation.

At the other end of the fuel system, clean fuel has to be supplied to the engine. With two tanks it should be possible to run the engine off either tank. If two engines are fitted then it should be possible to run either engine off either tank. This can be done with a system of piping and valves which can be adapted to suit the particular installation, but there are certain basic principles to be observed.

Each tank should have a shut-off valve mounted directly onto the tank. This allows the supply to be cut off in the event of a fire or leakage. These valves should be readily accessible, and it is good practice to extend the

Fig 24 The water intake and part of the fuel system on a small steel vessel. The fuel drain can be seen under the main fuel cock. Both the latter and the seacock would benefit by being extended to deck level.

spindles to deck level so that they can be turned off without the necessity of entering the engine compartment. These same valves can be used to select the tank to supply the engine, and as they should both feed into a common pipe they can be used to level off the tanks when filling or to maintain the trim.

With a single tank and engine the supply pipe is quite straightforward and only one shut-off valve is required. With two engines and two tanks the system is more complex. Valves in the fuel system should close positively, and the best are the screw down valves which give a good seal. The valves must be designed for handling the fuel concerned otherwise there will be trouble with the sealing materials. The taper valves which only require a 90° turn to switch them off are not generally satisfactory because after some wear they invariably leak. The drain-off valve on the fuel tank should be of the spring loaded type so that it cannot be opened accidentally.

Where fuel is carried in double bottom tanks a header tank is sometimes used in the engine compartment. This is fitted with level switches which automatically switch on a small electric pump to raise the fuel to the header tank. This arrangement can reduce the demands on the engine driven pump and ensure an adequate supply of fuel.

Although engines are now commonly fitted with their own fuel filters and separators, it is good practice to fit a water and sludge trap into the fuel line. The clear glass bowl of these units can give a good indication of the condition of the fuel. Diesel engines particularly require clean fuel. The glass bowl of this unit should be protected from accidental damage.

Fuel lines should be of metal. Copper is commonly used, and even when the engine is firmly mounted a coil should be introduced into the pipe to allow for vibration. Copper is prone to becoming brittle through continuous vibration and it is becoming common practice to fit a length of flexible pipe into the system to allow for any slight movement. Plastic pipe is not suitable for this purpose, even the reinforced type. It would quickly melt in the event of a fire and only the specially designed metal-covered flexible pipes should be used.

Fuel lines must be secured to prevent any movement. Where they have to be bent, the bend should be gentle to avoid kinking the pipe, and the pipe should not pass over sharp edges without suitable packing underneath. Pipes should not be placed where they might be trodden on or knocked, and if necessary they should be protected. Joints should be of the metal to metal type, and leaks must be eliminated. Apart from wasting fuel, a leak creates a fire risk.

It is advisable to keep fuel tanks topped up as much as possible, thus reducing the risk of condensation in the tank. Even so, it is advisable to have some means of measuring how much fuel remains in the tank. Sight gauges, where a clear plastic or glass tube is fitted to the tank connected to a metal fitting at top and bottom, are a simple means of checking the contents. They are practical, provided that they are fitted with a spring loaded shut-off valve at the top and bottom. These valves will close automatically except when a reading is being taken of the contents, so that damage to the sight tube does not mean loss of fuel.

These direct reading content gauges are simple, but have been largely superseded by a dial gauge which operates via float in the tank. There are two types, those with a mechanical linkage and those with an electrical linkage. The former is usually mounted on the tank itself, but the electrical type can be mounted in the wheelhouse if desired.

Gauges, in general, are not always accurate, especially when the boat is moving at sea. They are sensitive to trim and the readings should be used with caution. When calibrating a gauge it should always err on the side of showing less fuel in the tank than there actually is. A reliable method of checking the fuel in the tank is by means of a dipstick, which certainly has the merit of simplicity, but is not always easy to use at sea, because opening the filler cap to take a reading may allow water in.

It pays to keep a check on the fuel consumption. This can be a simple matter of installing an engine-hour meter and recording the amount of fuel taken on board. Once the average consumption has been established, it should be possible to detect any increase caused by a hidden fuel leak or an engine defect. As the cost of fuel rises, every effort should be made to conserve it.

Little maintenance is required on the fuel system, except regular inspections to ensure that all is well and changing filters at recommended intervals. Cleanliness of the fuel is of vital importance, and although a well installed system will clean dirty fuel, particular care should be taken to see that the fuel put into the tank is clean. This is essential where fishermen maintain their own fuel supplies ashore.

CHAPTER 4

Electrical Installation

Probably the most neglected part of any fishing boat is the electrical system. It is rare to find a really good installation even on a new boat yet the electrical system has now become a vital part of every fishing boat. It supplies power for engine starting, for navigation and other lighting and for the now vital electronic navigation and fish-finding equipment. Faults in the electrical system can result in any or all of these vital items not working, can introduce a fire hazard, and can be responsible for the onset of rot in a wooden hull or corrosion in a steel hull.

An electrical system which is well installed initially has a good chance of remaining reliable. Most of the problems on installation come from a failure to appreciate the demanding conditions under which the electrical system has to operate. Installation is often carried out by electricians who have little idea of the conditions at sea on a fishing boat. What might appear quite satisfactory in a boatyard may be totally unreliable when the boat is operating in rough seas.

The main consideration during installation, and also during any modification, is to make sure that water in any form cannot come into contact with the bare metal of the electrical circuit. Using modern plastic covered wires means that the wiring itself is generally safe from water, but where connections are made in junction boxes, switches and electrical fittings trouble can occur. At these points there are often dissimilar metals and if any water is present, corrosion can rapidly occur.

Even without the presence of dissimilar metals, corrosion will occur, particularly if the water present is salt water. Corrosion can have two effects; it may eat right through the metal and cause a break in the curcuit, or it may just build up a high resistance between two contacts so that the circuit becomes inoperative. The first problem is probably the worse of the two because the break in the circuit can lead to arcing, which can start a fire if there is any inflammable material nearby.

Water can enter the electrical system from many sources. Any electrical fittings on the deck or superstructure are exposed to the full force of flying spray which will soon penetrate even the slightest flaw in the defences. Electrical equipment fitted in the wheelhouse is normally fairly well protected. However, windows are a potential source of leaks and water may be carried into the wheelhouse on wet oilskins. In this case the water is more likely to drip onto fittings rather than be driven with any force, but the result will be the same unless the fittings are designed to keep the water out.

Wiring in the fish hold and in stores is exposed to a very damp atmosphere which can be very harmful and neither the engine compartment nor the accommodation is immune in this respect. When the engine is running and the accommodation is being used they will keep fairly dry, but when the boat is left at moorings there can be a great deal of condensation in those areas, which can run down the bulkheads or the ship's side and find its way into the electrical fittings.

There is also the problem of damage to the electrical system through vibration and wear. Careful installation of the wiring is the only way this can be avoided, but it needs someone who can really appreciate the problems if a satisfactory result is to be obtained.

The heart of the electrical system is the battery or batteries. The engine-driven generator feeds electrical current into the battery and the power is then available for distribution around the vessel. If the battery

Fig 25   The electrical fittings placed close to this air intake will corrode rapidly with the salt laden air coming in.

48

installation is not satisfactory then the rest of the system will not be either.

There are two types of battery in use on boats. The lead acid battery is in almost universal use. These are the same as those used in cars and trucks and give good reliable service provided that they are well maintained. They do require regular charging which is usually no problem on a fishing boat. If left unattended for a long time they lose their charge, so that for a fishing boat which is in seasonal use, it may be preferable to use alkaline batteries.

Alkaline batteries usually have nickel cadmium plates and there are two types, low resistance and normal resistance. The former is suitable for providing the heavy currents required for engine starting, while the latter is better suited to providing the long term moderate loads used for lighting. Alkaline batteries are more expensive than the lead acid type, but in their favour is the fact that they can have a useful working life of up to ten years, much more than the average lead acid battery.

The very low losses from an alkaline battery when it is left idle can give improved reliability and reduce the likelihood of a flat battery on starting. They can also be charged at a higher rate than lead acid batteries. In spite of these advantages, it is usually initial cost which is the over-riding factor and on this score the lead acid battery is almost invariably preferred. Probably also in favour of the lead acid battery is the fact that most fishermen know and understand it because it is the type fitted in their cars and trucks.

With either type of battery, installation is similar except that an alkaline battery requires a steel drip tray and a lead acid battery should have a lead tray. These materials are chosen to prevent corrosion if the electrolyte is spilt, but in many cases the tray is made from GRP or metal or wood coated with this material, which is both simpler and cheaper. The tray should be capable of containing any electrolyte which might be spilt when testing the batteries, or through bubbling when the batteries are being charged. It should also be strong enough to support the weight of the batteries and to locate them securely so that they cannot move when the boat rolls.

On small craft where the boat movement can sometimes be particularly violent the batteries should be secured so that they cannot come out of the tray. This may sound extreme, but during a heavy roll the high inertia of the batteries could cause them to fall out. In bad sea conditions the loss of electrical power can be fatal.

There must be no movement of the batteries in the tray at all. Even slight movement will cause continual flexing of the heavy cables leading to the starter motor, and eventually these will be weakened or will break. Under these circumstances, there is a real danger of fire and it will not be possible to start the engine.

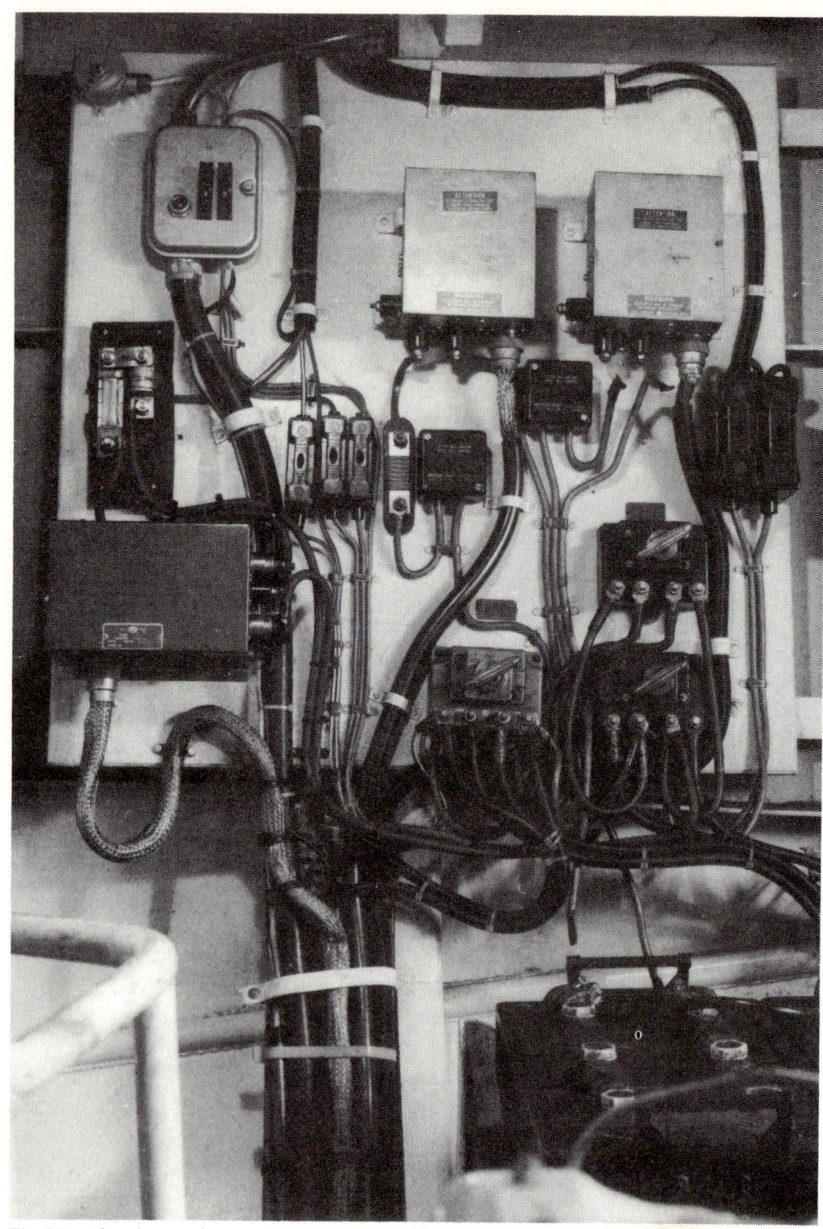

Fig 26   The electrical system on a large trawler with a single engine showing the battery
stowage bottom right.

The batteries must be installed in an accessible position where they can be serviced easily. Only in this way will they get the attention they deserve. Servicing is simply a matter of topping up the electrolyte and occasionally checking the state of charge with a hydrometer. The tops of the batteries should be kept clean and dry so that there is a reduced possibility of short circuiting between the outlet terminals. Modern batteries have the inter-cell connections moulded in below the top of the battery surface so that these cannot contribute to such a leakage and this also makes it much easier to keep the battery clean.

The batteries should be placed where they will not be affected by spray or rain even when the engine hatches are open. Provision must be made to ventilate the area above the batteries to remove the dangerous hydrogen gas produced during charging. This gas is lighter than air and can collect in pockets over the battery area. A spark could cause a violent explosion, so in general, electrical apparatus should be kept away from the area above the batteries.

If the batteries are contained in a box this must be provided with an air vent to the deck from the top of the box and an inlet at the bottom. On large battery installations it is good practice to fit an electrically driven fan to give positive ventilation and this is interlocked with the charging circuit so that it is running automatically whenever the batteries are being charged. Good ventilation of the batteries will also help to keep them cool, which will prolong their life.

Switches should not be placed in any battery compartment because of the danger from sparks, and smoking should never be allowed when attending the batteries. The danger of the hydrogen gas emitted from batteries is not generally appreciated, and lack of simple safety precautions has led to several nasty accidents.

On all but the smallest boats, more than one battery is used. These can be connected in different ways to meet different requirements. Most modern diesel engines use a 24 volt system. To obtain this voltage it is usual to connect two 12 volt batteries in series. Two heavy duty 12 volt batteries are usually sufficient to meet the electrical requirements of a small boat, but these requirements increase with increasing size of the boat, so the batteries are divided up to keep the individual units to a manageable size. Perhaps four 6 volt batteries would be connected in series on larger craft.

The size of battery required for a particular boat is usually dictated by the engine starting requirements. A battery which will be suitable for the type of engine in use will generally be suitable to supply the other electrical requirements of the boat. If these are particularly heavy, the capacity of the batteries should be increased so that there is a good margin in case of a charging failure, or for use in port when the engine is not running.

A modern development in battery systems uses two banks of batteries for one engine. Both batteries are charged from one alternator, the charge being directed to the battery which requires most charging by means of a blocking diode. This is a simple electronic device which is reliable and requires no maintenance. This system allows one battery to be maintained fully charged for engine starting while the other is used for the auxiliary circuits. The roles of the batteries can be reversed, and in this way both batteries could be run down when the charging system is not operative. This is not easy to do accidentally, and the fact that batteries have had to be switched to maintain the supply should give sufficient warning that too much power is being used.

Even when both batteries have been used in this way, a switch can be incorporated in the battery circuits which allows the two batteries to be temporarily connected in series so that it may be possible to get sufficient voltage to start the engine.

Battery charging at sea is usually no problem and a single engine-driven alternator should be sufficient to supply most requirements. In many cases it is possible to increase the size of the engine-driven alternator from the standard, or alternatively a larger alternator can be driven from the power take-off on the front of the engine, or be belt driven from the propeller shaft.

In the quest to secure the utmost in reliability, two alternators with independent driving sources should be considered. It is probably much better to spend more time and effort in making a single alternator charging system reliable. After all, the boat is not put out of action entirely if the battery is not being charged. There should be sufficient capacity in the batteries to maintain the essential services for some time.

Many older boats still use dynamos instead of alternators to produce their electrical power. The dynamo produces direct current which can be fed directly to the batteries *via* a cut-out. The cut-out prevents the battery charge from feeding back to the dynamo when the latter is not charging. The disadvantage of the dynamo is that it does not supply a current at slow speeds and long periods of engine idling could lead to flat batteries.

The alternator can produce its current at very low speeds, but the current it produces is alternating and has to be rectified into direct current before it can be fed to the batteries. The rectifier is generally incorporated into the alternator body. The alternator is generally a very reliable unit which requires little maintenance. There is little difference in cost between an alternator and a dynamo and all modern engines are fitted with alternators. Many fishing boats have modernized their charging systems by replacing the dynamo with an alternator.

The electrical system may be used a considerable amount when the vessel is in harbour with a consequent heavy drain on the batteries. If it is possible to bring a shore supply to the boat, there are charging units available which will automatically maintain the batteries at a full state of charge. These units are well worth considering as a permanent installation on the boat.

Alternatively, if shore power is available in the boat's normal berth, a separate electrical system could be installed on the boat working on the shore supply voltage. However, such separate systems can be dangerous because the high voltage involved can give lethal shocks as well as start fires. The installation of the circuits must be very carefully done and there must be no possibility of any of the fittings getting wet.

The same applies to the 110 volt circuits used on some of the larger boats. This voltage can be dangerous and extra care is required. The higher voltage is used to supply the domestic lighting and power requirements which, on a larger boat, can be considerable. By using a higher voltage the current consumption is less, so that the wiring size is kept to manageable proportions.

Direct current is normally used in connection with the 110 volt circuit because it is much simpler to control and distribute than alternating current. Because there is a greater chance of arcing in switches and other fittings with direct current these fittings have to be selected from specially designed ranges. Many of the household electrical fittings which it is tempting to use because of their cheapness, are not suitable because they are designed only for alternating currents.

The highest voltage which can be conveniently used in connection with a bank of batteries is about 110 volts. If batteries are included in the circuit, as is often the case for use in harbour, then it is essential to use direct current.

Modern battery charging systems connected to engine driven power units are completely automatic in operation. In a 24 volt system where the alternator first supplies alternating current, this is rectified into direct current, often within the alternator itself. The control circuits then regulate the load supplied by the alternator to the batteries to match both the state of charge of the batteries and the load on the various circuits which the batteries supply.

An ammeter should always be included in the charging circuit to show that all is well or to indicate a fault. Often a charging light is included to show that the alternator is charging. The ammeter shows the balance between the current going into the battery and the current being taken out.

If there are no circuits switched on and the engine has just been started to get ready for sea, the ammeter will show a high reading on the charge side as the alternator strives to replace the heavy current used for the starter motor. After a short while the reading will drop as the battery regains its charge and the charging rate is automatically reduced.

Switching on equipment at this stage should not affect the ammeter greatly, although it may vary slightly as the automatic control makes the balance. During normal running the alternator should be able to match the operating load and the ammeter should show a slight charge. If there is a heavy load, the ammeter may show a discharge which means that the battery is losing power. This is acceptable for a short while or when the engine is idling and the charging rate is less, but in the long term it indicates that the alternator is not capable of coping with the load and flat batteries will result.

A steady high discharge when the engine is running usually indicates a fault in the charging circuits as the ammeter is showing the current being used by the equipment in use, but this is not being replaced by the alternator. This may be a fault in the alternator or the control circuits, but is more likely to be a slipping or broken driving belt to the alternator, or a blown fuse in the charging circuits. These are simple to check.

All charging circuits should be protected by a fuse, but even this is unlikely to prevent damage to the alternator if the battery is disconnected while the alternator is running. It is common to fit battery isolating switches in the main cables from the batteries. These cut out all the circuits from the battery and prevent any leakage of current when the boat is left idle. The engine cannot be started until these switches have been closed but they must not be touched when the engine is running. These heavy duty swtiches are often combined with the battery change-over and interconnecting switches.

The power cables for all the auxiliary circuits are taken from the batteries to a distribution box where the circuits divide to provide the various services required. Each individual circuit is protected by a fuse of appropriate rating, although it is now possible to replace fuses by a circuit breaker which will open the circuit in the event of an overload. These circuit breakers are better than fuses as it is simply a matter of pressing them in again to close the circuit. If they stay closed the circuit is still in order and it was simply an intermittent overload or vibration which caused them to open. Vibration can be a problem with circuit breakers. Because they are spring loaded they can be affected by heavy vibration and can open the circuit even though there is no fault. This is more liable to happen in a rough sea, but against this must be weighed the advantage that it is much easier to restore the circuit than by fitting a new fuse, and better designs are overcoming this defect.

The circuits on the boat can be divided up into convenient groupings. The navigation lights may be on one circuit, the deck lights on another, the fish hold lights and accommodation lights having further circuits. Power circuits where there is a heavier loading should be kept separate from lighting circuits, and there should be a separate circuit for each piece of electronic equipment in the wheelhouse.

The distribution board or box is located either in the wheelhouse or the engine compartment, depending on the layout of the boat. The wheelhouse is more convenient when it comes to replacing a fuse, but whatever the location, it must be in a position where it will remain dry. It is difficult to make a distribution box watertight because of the many wires leading into it, and the multitude of contacts inside can cause much damage if water gets in.

If the distribution box is placed in the engine compartment, it must be under cover and not near the edge of hatches where water is likely to drip on it. The engine may have to be serviced at sea with the hatches open, so the box and all the other electrical equipment in the engine compartment must be well protected.

The wiring used on a boat should always be of the stranded copper type. This is much more flexible than solid wire and is not so liable to fracture through movement or vibration which will always be present on a boat, no matter how carefully the wire is secured. Clips for wires should be spaced about every six inches (10 cm) and the clips should be secured by screws or bolts, not nails. There is a risk of damaging the wire insulation when the nails are hammered in. Screws or bolts should be brass or stainless steel to reduce corrosion. The clips can be of brass but it is now much more common to use plastic.

The alternative to clipping the wire in place is to contain it in conduit. The old type steel conduit suffered from corrosion very quickly even though it may be galvanized, but modern plastic conduit is immune to corrosion and very simple to install. Apart from avoiding the time-consuming need to secure cables, plastic conduit offers protection to the cables, but it can make the tracing of faults more difficult because the wires cannot be traced inside the conduit unless they are colour coded. Plastic conduit must be carefully located so that it does not provide a convenient handhold where it bridges two deck beams or a similar space. It is not strong enough to be so used and the possibility should be avoided.

It is prudent to include provision for additional electrical circuits for future use. Additional lights and equipment, particularly in the electronics field, may be required at a later date, and where the wire is carried in conduit it is worth the cost to include some extra wires, particularly to the wheelhouse.

The insulation on the wire used on the electrical circuits is now normally

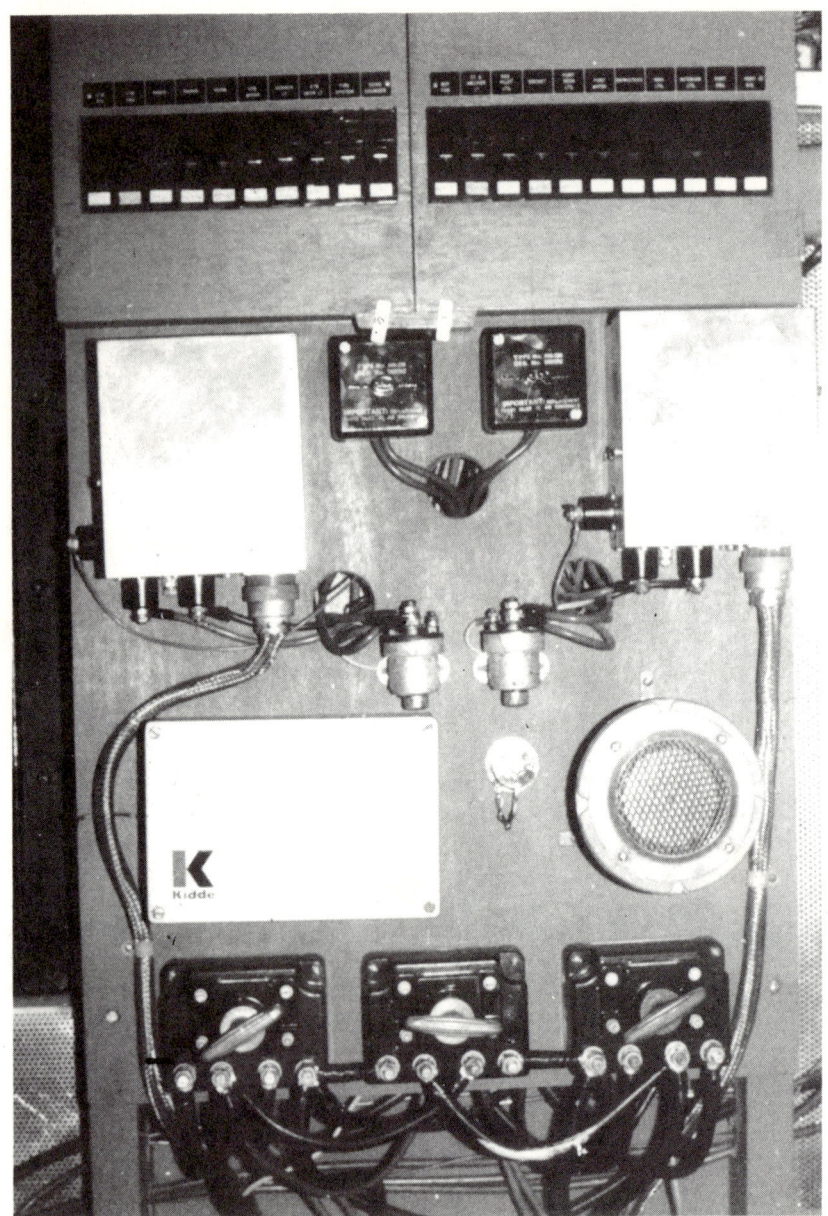

Fig 27   A twin engine electrical installation showing the main battery switches at the bottom and the distribution board at the top.

butyl rubber, which is a synthetic rubber with good wear resistance properties and is immune to attack by oil, moderate heat and sea water. For added protection it can be sheathed in polyvinylchloride but this is not normally required where conduit is in use. The cross-sectional area of the copper wire determines the amount of current which it can safely carry, and this rating should never be exceeded. In fact it is preferable to allow a margin because heavier current loadings may be required at a later date.

Cable runs should be as straight as possible because trouble usually starts at the bends. Where the cable enters a fitting it should enter from the bottom so that any moisture which might run along the cable cannot enter the fitting. If the wire has to run horizontally or downwards towards the fitting then a small downward loop should be introduced just before the fitting so that the water will drip off. This applies to fittings both inside and outside. Even with watertight glands fitted, water collecting on the outside of the gland will eventually find its way in, if left there continually.

Engine compartment and accommodation fittings should be placed clear of portholes and openings where they might be exposed to spray or rain driving in. Even then they should be fitted where they are protected as far as possible from water such as condensation draining downwards. This can often find its way into the back of fittings and cause havoc, giving little or no indication until the circuit fails to work.

Some fittings are advertised as splashproof which means that a spray of water coming from above will not affect them, but these units are not always proof against the general damp corrosive atmosphere which is found in some areas of a boat. Lights in the fish hold, for instance, must be fully watertight and generally must be protected against mechanical damage as well when fish boxes or pound boards are being moved about.

Areas such as the steering gear compartment can also become very damp from condensation or because damp gear is stowed there. The wheelhouse is another area where damp from a variety of sources can occur as already mentioned, and it is wise to use fully watertight electrical fittings. The dashboard on smaller boats is often the cause of trouble because the switches mounted in the panel are often not watertight and water can find its way through the top of the switches into the electrical contacts underneath.

The switches on the dashboard often control important circuits such as the navigation and compass lights. The dashboard may look tidy with all the wiring carefully hidden away underneath, but on many boats it is a source of trouble. When water has found its way behind the panel and starts off corrosion it is often difficult to gain access, particularly if the boat is at sea. To make matters worse this is the site often chosen for the electrical distribution and fuse box, at least for the wheelhouse circuits, largely because it minimizes the wiring visible in the wheelhouse. It would

Fig 28 A neat electric navigation light. A downward loop is put into the wire to reduce the chance of water getting into the gland at the base.

be much better to have these units mounted on a bulkhead where they are readily accessible. Most of the switches could be moved as well and still remain close at hand.

Most people realize the obvious necessity to keep outside electrical fittings watertight. Even then there are certain methods which can lead to a more reliable installation. Having a half-loop in a wire before it enters a watertight gland can prevent water lying in the gland, as already suggested. Glands should be at the bottom of fittings, and, where watertight sockets are necessary, they are best mounted on overhanging surfaces where they will have better protection. The wires leaving these sockets are always vulnerable and it is not unusual to see the insulation cracked around the place where the wire leaves the gland, a sure sign of trouble to come.

Try to mount the sockets where they and the wires coming out of them will be protected. These sockets have watertight caps to replace the plug when it is removed and these should always be fitted, otherwise new sockets will have to be fitted at frequent intervals. It should not be necessary to have many watertight sockets on a fishing boat; in many cases the wire can be led inboard through a gland thus reducing the number of connections and trouble spots.

Outside lights are required and there are some excellent units available specifically designed for the purpose. These are not only watertight, but they are also designed to withstand the considerable vibration which can occur particularly on masts and gantrys. It is false economy to use cheap fittings in these locations. There is increasing use of fluorescent lighting both for deck lighting and internally. The higher initial cost of these units

Fig 29 A good electrical fitting even to the extent of providing a stowage for the socket cover when the socket is in use.

is off-set by their greater efficiency. They use less power for the same amount of light and have a longer life, particularly where there is vibration, because they have no filaments.

Fluorescent lights can cause radio interference. They may have to be fitted with suppressors, and so should not be installed close to the radios. Other equipment may also require suppressing and if radio interference is present, the offending units can be found by switching on each electrical apparatus one at a time. Suppression is effected by connecting condensers from the input terminals to earth, which reduces the current surge, but this is the work of a skilled electrician.

Interference can also be reduced by earthing all the electrical apparatus. This will also eliminate any stray electrical currents caused by damp or short circuits which can be the cause of structural decay, particularly in wooden boats. These currents can set up a potential difference between two metal fittings in the hull and the damp wood of the hull can act as the return path of the circuit which causes rot in the timber, particularly around the metal fittings.

It is to avoid setting up currents in the hull that double wiring is always used. The current is then carried out and back by wire and the hull of a metal boat is not used as the return path. Earthing wires should also be insulated to prevent the currents draining off into the structure.

Particular care has to be taken with 110 volt or shore supply circuits. Any leakage of these circuits to earth can cause very rapid corrosion or decay.

The electrical system of a boat is complicated and there are a great many factors to take into account. While an electrician can be relied on to carry out an efficient installation which will work satisfactorily in the boatyard, he may not appreciate all the factors which go towards making an installation which is efficient at sea. He may tend to put the fittings where there is a convenient space rather than looking for protected areas, and the electrical system could greatly benefit by being taken into consideration during the design stages of the boat.

Whether the electrical system is being installed on a new boat or that on an existing boat is being modified or extended, it is the owner's ultimate responsibility to ensure that the final result is satisfactory. This chapter should provide an insight into some of the problems involved and help in making a critical appraisal of the installation.

CHAPTER 5

Auxiliary Systems

There is a tendency to regard the auxiliary systems on a fishing boat such as the hydraulic system, the pumping system and possibly refrigeration, as being of less importance than the main engine and to treat their installation and maintenance in a casual manner. Yet if the hydraulic system fails it will not be possible for the boat to fish; without the pumping system the boat may sink, and if the refrigeration system fails, the catch may be ruined. All of these occurrences are detrimental to the prime objective of a fishing boat, which is to earn money from fishing.

The advantage of having two propulsion engines has already been mentioned and the same approach should be adopted with the auxiliary systems so that, as far as possible, the failure of any one unit will not put the boat out of action. This is another reason for having two engines: each one can be used to drive separate auxiliary systems.

Instead of having two propulsion engines, on larger boats it is common to have a separate engine for driving the auxiliary systems such as hydraulic pumps, bilge and deck wash pumps and generators. It is prudent to include some provision for this engine to be connected to the main propeller shaft, so that it could be used for propulsion in an emergency.

Probably the simplest connection would be a form of belt drive from the auxiliary engine direct to pulleys on the propeller shaft. An alternative would be to have an hydraulic motor connected to the winch hydraulic system, which could be used to turn the shaft. Much would depend on the layout of a particular vessel, but this alternative is well worth considering.

Such a system would be used in emergencies only. It would only give very slow speeds because of the limited power available, and should be used for returning to port rather than for use to continue fishing in the event of an engine failure. Whether the expense of installing such a system is justified can only be decided on the particular fishing methods employed.

Auxiliary engines are installed in much the same way as the main propulsion engine and should be given the same care and attention. Air-cooled engines are often used, particularly if the vessel operates from a harbour which dries out. This allows the engine to be operated even when the boat is high and dry.

Another method is to use an engine with a fresh water cooling system and have the water cooled by a radiator with a fan blowing air over it. This is the same system used in trucks so that conversion to marine use of the engine is not required. This has the advantage of low cost. The only modification which might be required is fitting a larger capacity fan, and the radiator carefully located to ensure a good flow of cool air through it.

Whether the auxiliaries are driven from the main engine or from an auxiliary engine, the problems involved are similar, except that driving auxiliaries directly from the front of the main engine increases its overall length. This can decrease the space available for the fish hold, which may not be acceptable. This is one of the main reasons why

Fig 30 A layshaft driven from the main engine used to drive twin pumps. A separate drive just visible drives an hydraulic pump.

auxiliaries are usually mounted on each side of the engine and driven by belts from the crankshaft pulley. Belt-driven auxiliaries put a considerable extra stress on both the crankshaft bearings and on the bearings of the unit being driven because of the sideways thrust involved. There is much less stress on the bearings when a unit is directly driven.

In all cases of drives being taken from the front of the engine, the engine manufacturers will state the power which can be used in this way, either as a percentage of the total horsepower or more directly as the horsepower available. The total horsepower of the units being driven has to be calculated and a considerable allowance of up to 20% added for the power absorbed by the drive system. The direct drive absorbs less power than a belt drive.

When considering the fitting of auxiliaries, the operating speed of the auxiliary unit must be considered and whether it can be run continuously. An alternator is designed to run within the speed range of the engine and, in fact, is usually geared so that it runs at a higher speed. A pump may run satisfactorily at varying engine speeds, but while it may produce a good jet for deck washing at full engine speed, it may only produce a trickle at idling speeds. Both water pumps and hydraulic pumps are a particular problem in this respect and this is often why an auxiliary engine is installed on many boats, so that pumps can be driven at a constant speed for maximum efficiency. Where the drive must be taken off the main engine, the engine speed required when it operates deck machinery or pumps has to be decided and the drive ratio for the pump selected accordingly.

On most boats a fairly low running speed is selected, so that the engine can be taken in or out of gear to manoeuvre the boat while the fishing gear is being hauled. The output can be varied by altering engine speed within limits, and a clutch is fitted to each unit so that it can be disconnected from its drive when the boat is under way.

Some units are more flexible than others with regard to driving speed and this is an important point to consider when selecting equipment. To leave a unit running when the power is not required leads to increased wear, and on hydraulic pumps can lead to an increase in the hydraulic oil temperature. Some types of water pump require a flow of water to lubricate them adequately, so these should never be allowed to run dry.

While belt drive is now the most commonly used system for driving auxiliaries, many conversions carried out by fishermen have utilized components derived from truck or car transmission systems. Provided that they are properly engineered there is no reason why these should not work effectively. One obvious way to take the drive

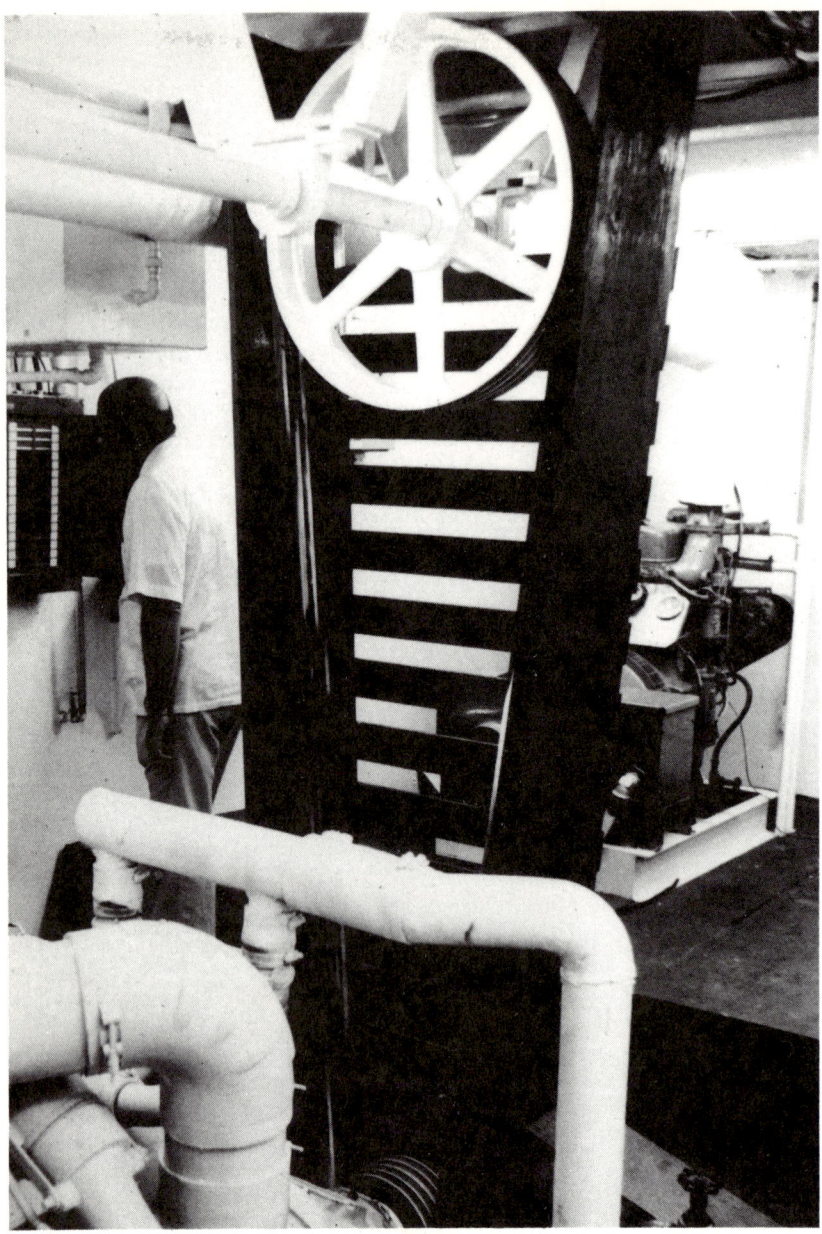

Fig 31   A belt drive for a winch taken from the power take off at the front of the main engine.
The auxiliary generator and pump can be seen behind.

Fig 32   Twin alternators fitted to supply the high power requirements of a fishing boat. The other belt drive supplies the hydraulic pump.

65

from the front end of an engine would be to utilize a truck rear axle, connecting the centre drive to the crankshaft and driving the auxiliaries from each end. The reduction ratio in the axle must be taken into account when calculating the drive ratio. It may be possible to use gearboxes to alter the ratio.

These components have been used in various forms to connect a mechanical drive from the engine to the deck machinery. Before the advent of hydraulic systems, mechanical drives were common, the usual system being to have a long driving belt from the crankshaft pulley to a layshaft at deck level which was used to drive the winch. These systems were generally unreliable owing to belt slip, and indeed slipping the belt was often the only means of disconnecting the drive. The often exposed belts and shafts were dangerous to men working near them, and such drives are less common on new boats today.

A mechanical drive for the deck machinery is still probably the least costly type of drive system and if properly installed it can operate satisfactorily. A clutch should be fitted at the engine end of the system so that the shafts and belts are not turning continuously. This clutch, if of the plate type, could also be used as the means of control for the drive. Correct alignment of the bearings is essential for long life of the drive system and provision must be made for adequate lubrication. One of the main problems with mechanical drives is that the shafts and bearings are often hidden away and lack maintenance.

One of the main advantages of hydraulic drive for deck machinery is flexibility in locating the various pieces of equipment because all connections are made by flexible pressure hose which is simple to install. Like any piping on board a fishing boat, the hydraulic hose should be fixed securely to avoid any movement which might lead to wear on the pipe. These pipes are subjected to very high pressure and a leak could be dangerous.

The flexible pipes withstand sea water very well but should be examined occasionally for signs of wear and deterioration. The joints at the end of the pipes seem to suffer most. These hydraulic hoses are designed for general purposes and not specifically for marine use, consequently the metal unions at the end of the pipes are not corrosion proof and deteriorate very quickly unless they are carefully painted.

The normal hydraulic system used on a fishing boat is an open system where the oil is drawn from a reservoir to the pump. After passing through the system the used oil is returned to the reservoir which is not under pressure. The reservoir holds a large quantity of oil which helps to dissipate the heat generated in the system through friction. When none of the deck machinery is running, a by-pass valve circulates the oil between the pump and the reservoir only. Where heat building up in the oil is a particular problem, a cooler can be introduced into the system whereby the oil is cooled by means of a sea water circulation. Such a cooler is often fitted into the reservoir itself, particularly when available space only allows a small reservoir to be fitted.

The alternative to the open hydraulic system is the closed system, where the whole system is under pressure and the oil is continuously circulated around a distribution pipe and the supply to the various units is controlled by valves. This system utilizes a much higher pressure than the open system, possibly around 2000 lb/sq in and is more efficient. It needs very careful installation and a cooler is essential because of the relatively small amount of oil in circulation.

Cleanliness inside the hydraulic system is essential. Not only are particles of dirt likely to prevent the valves working properly, but they will lead to rapid wear in the motors and pump. When first installed the pipes must be carefully flushed out. The oil put into the system must be clean, and as an additional precaution, a filter or filters are fitted into the system.

Many manufacturers of hydraulic deck machinery supply a hydraulic pump with the unit so that the pump and drive motor are matched satisfactorily. This is satisfactory where only one deck unit is used but if there are several units fitted, then unnecessary complications can arise if a separate pump is supplied for each unit.

Trawlers will often use other deck machinery at the same time as the main trawl winch. Such items as the net drum and the transducer coiler may also be hydraulically driven, in which case the system has to be designed to cope with the varying load.

The design of hydraulic systems is for the specialist, particularly for control gear. Sophisticated valves can enable the operator to have very precise control over the hydraulic equipment, and the fisherman should specify his exact requirements to the designer. For instance, he may require a line hauler which will haul at a faster rate when the load is light, reducing the rate of haul as the load increases. If a continuous rate of haul is required irrespective of load, the control system can provide this, with the rate being adjusted by variation in the driving engine speed.

The type of pump and motor will also affect the characteristics of the system. The gear pump (and its modern counterpart the screw pump), the centrifugal pump and the vane pump are in general use, and except for the centrifugal pump, these can also be adapted as motors. High pressure systems often use axial or radial piston pumps, which are more complex but provide better control as the capacity of the pump can be altered. These are the variable displacement pumps and motors as opposed to the constant displacement types mentioned earlier.

Fig 33 A hydraulic control valve which will control speed and direction of rotation.

The screw pump is commonly used on modern low pressure installations. The pump and its equivalent motor are compact and well balanced and have a long life with little maintenance. The centrifugal pump is also long lasting because there are no internal wearing surfaces, as is the case with the vane pump and motor. The vane motor is used frequently for driving winches where it can be mounted directly onto the main shaft of the winch without any gearing.

On small fishing boats where the additional expense of fitting dual hydraulic systems may be unacceptable, a simple system can be devised which is easy to adapt to the different methods of fishing which these craft often undertake throughout the seasons. Such different methods require (at different times) a power block, a trawl winch and a line hauler. It may be possible to combine the first and the last in one unit, but even if it is not, it is possible to have one hydraulic motor to drive each unit in turn as the seasons progress. In this way all that is required is an engine driven pump and one motor with its control valve, representing a considerable saving of costs.

Alternative drive systems for deck machinery are pneumatic and electric. Pneumatic drive is very similar to hydraulic except that the air is not re-circulated. Gearing is required to reduce the speed of the driving turbines which adds to the complication. Probably the biggest disadvantage is the noise created by the exhausted air. Unless complex silencers are fitted this noise is objectionable and largely accounts for the preference for a hydraulic drive system.

Electric drive is sometimes used on larger craft but is not popular on smaller fishing boats, partly because more space is required for the generators and driving motors and partly because the high voltages and currents involved make the system particularly susceptible to damage by water. An electric motor will occupy about five times the space of an hydraulic motor of similar power, thus occupying valuable deck space on a small boat.

Lack of space is probably the main reason why refrigeration has not been widely adopted for small fishing boats. The refrigeration machinery requires a considerable amount of space and the power necessary can be large. Few small boats stay at sea long enough to justify freezing the catch, and preparation for freezing requires both time and space, both of which can usually be put to better use in catching fish.

Ice is the normal means of keeping the catch in good condition if the boat is at sea for more than 24 hours. The ice is loaded before sailing and can keep the fish hold cool for several days provided the hold is well insulated. The volume of the ice restricts the amount of fish which can be accommodated, but during the voyage the ice melts and is pumped away leaving more space for the fish.

On small fishing boats there may be a case for a small refrigeration plant, not to freeze the catch, but to help keep the fish hold cool and prolong the effectiveness of the ice. It need not be large and the compressor could be belt driven from the main or auxiliary engine. By using a fan blowing air over the cooling pipes, the cold air could be distributed around the fish hold and this circulation of air would help to keep the hold fresh.

An alternative to loading large quantities of ice is to have an ice making machine on board. These are normally electrically powered, but hydraulically driven models are available. It is easier to use fresh water to make the ice because it is less corrosive, but modern plants can use sea or fresh water, whichever is available. This puts less pressure on the fresh water supplies on board. By making ice on board, only as much as is needed is produced and there is no wastage, but it adds to complication of the machinery fitted.

The bilge pumping system is used to remove melted ice from the fish hold and this must be carefully designed if it is to be effective at all times. Some sections of the bilge pumping system will rarely be used except in an emergency when there may be a leak in the hull.

The main part of the bilge pumping system is the pump itself. Various types are used such as centrifugal, piston, gear and vane pumps. The centrifugal pump is satisfactory provided it can be run at a constant speed as with a drive from an auxiliary engine, but it is unsuitable for use with the main engine due to its varying speed. An advantage of the centrifugal pump is the low rate of wear because there are no rubbing surfaces except the bearings.

The piston pump is less popular because it is not suitable for removing dirty water which can cause the valves to remain open. It is also prone to rapid wear when there is much silt in the water. The same applies to the gear pump which relies on two gear wheels meshing and close tolerance between these and the housing to maintain pumping efficiency. Rubber coated gear wheels have been used to reduce the wear rate when there is silt in the water, but then an extra pair of driving pinions is required, thus reducing the simplicity of the design.

The vane type pump is now in general use as a bilge deck wash pump on small fishing boats. This type has an impeller with flexible vanes which is rotated off-centre in a metal (normally bronze) housing. Because it is off-centre the shape of the chambers formed by the vanes is continually varying causing the pumping action. Because the pump is of the positive displacement type it will continue to supply a water flow at low engine speeds and the amount of water delivered will vary directly with engine speed.

The impeller on such pumps is made from neoprene rubber which has a good resistance to both sea water and abrasion. The pumps are designed so that it is easy to replace the impeller, although the wear rate is fairly low provided that the pump is not run dry. If this happens the friction between the impeller and the casing will rapidly melt the rubber making a replacement imperative.

With bilge pumping there is always the risk of the pump running dry as the compartment is emptied. The discharge can be watched and the pump switched off when the flow stops. It is preferable to arrange for a small bleed pipe from the sea water intake to be connected to the pump so that even if the main suction dries up there will always be a small flow to keep the pump lubricated. There will be a loss of efficiency with this method, but this is offset by the reduction in the risk of the pump burning out.

On some boats the pump is arranged to run continuously with no clutch fitted between the pump and the engine. The valves are normally kept open for the deck wash system so that there is a constant flow, or the bleed system just described is used. In either case there will be increased wear on the pump and a waste of engine power so that it would be prudent to fit a clutch.

The clutch may be on the engine shaft if the pump is the only auxiliary fitted, but more usually it is incorporated in the pump housing so that the pump driving pulley runs freely when not pumping. This will increase belt wear, but this is not generally a serious problem. The clutch can be either of the simple mechanical type using either a dog, cone or plate or it can be a magnetic clutch which allows electrical control of the clutch from a remote position.

A good marine pump requires little maintenance except occasional checking and greasing. The checks largely involve looking at the drive belt for wear and checking for leaks. The same simple maintenance is all that is required for the pipe and valve system – oiling the valve spindles to ensure that they work freely and checking the pipes, particularly on the suction side, for leaks.

The bilge pumping system is normally made from metal pipes because in the event of a fire, flexible pipes could melt making the system inoperative when it is most needed. Galvanized steel pipes are often used in conjunction with bronze valves, but this could lead to corrosion problems if the pipes are left full of water. A combination of bronze valves and copper pipes would be better, but is more expensive.

The normal bilge pumping system connects the suction side of the pump to a valve chest or manifold. To this are connected the suction pipes to each of the individual compartments, each with its own shut-off valve and non-return valve. The shut-off valves enable the particular compartment to be pumped to be selected and the non-return valves prevent that compartment from being accidentally filled if the wrong valves are left open.

The valve manifold is also connected to a sea suction pipe which is why the non-return valves are fitted into the bilge lines. This sea suction enables the pump to be used to supply a flow of water for deck washing and other duties, and for this purpose the outlet from the pump can be varied. One outlet takes the flow of bilge water directly overboard. This pipe should have a non-return valve fitted at the point where it passes through the hull so that water cannot flow back down the pipe if valves are left open or if the pipe itself fractures or leaks.

The other outlet from the pump is led up to a convenient point on deck where a hose is connected for deck washing or fire fighting. On larger boats there may be more than one deck point, in which case they must be valve controlled. A simple system may not incorporate a bilge discharge and it may be necessary to utilize the deck wash hose hung overboard as the bilge discharge.

Because of the importance of the pumping system in emergencies, both for bilge pumping and for fire fighting, a hand pump is often incorporated into the system so that the same suctions and deliveries can be operated by the hand pump should the engine driven pump fail or the engine itself stop. The hand pump is fitted into the system in parallel to the engine driven pump with a valve in the line. The pump itself is usually mounted on deck so that it is easily accessible.

As an extra precaution a separate hand bilge pump is sometimes fitted with a suction directly to the engine compartment. This is the area most prone to leaks and this emergency pump can be used if the other system cannot be operated for any reason. Many boats also fit small electric bilge pumps which will operate automatically. These pumps are totally enclosed and are mounted directly into the bilge itself, the pump inlet being the suction pipe.

An automatic float switch can be incorporated into the circuit so that the pump will switch itself on if the water level rises above a pre-determined point. The pump will switch itself off again once the level has dropped. These pumps are very suitable for fitting to boats where there is a slight leakage, perhaps through the stern gland, or on wooden boats where the seams are not completely tight. The fitting of such a pump should only be regarded as a temporary solution to these problems.

The capacity of these electric pumps is generally fairly small, perhaps a maximum of 20 gallons/min so they are unlikely to cope with the failure of an engine cooling pipe or similar disaster when the boat is unattended. They will certainly help to keep the flow in check and the automatic switch could be connected to a flashing warning light on the mast which might bring help in time to prevent a foundering.

Another use for these automatic electric bilge pumps is in the fish hold sump. Because it may often be difficult to see what the water level in the hold is, an automatic pump could be arranged to pump out at a preset level, thus always keeping the hold clear. The only weakness of this system is that the pump may not be able to cope with some of the slurry found in the hold because of the small diameter of the suction pipes.

The electrical connection for these bilge pumps should be made so that they are not disconnected when the battery isolating switch is turned off. They should have their own separate circuit direct to the battery and a fuse is essential in the line. There is always the risk of the fuse blowing and the pump not working, but against this must be weighed the fire risk.

Whatever type of pump is fitted, the bilge pipe lines must be of adequate size to avoid restricting the flow. The size of the outlets on the pump will give a good indication of what it can handle, but another way to find an adequate size is to use the formula:

$$\text{diameter in inches} = \frac{\text{length of boat in feet}}{100} + 1$$

This gives a minimum diameter of one inch and a steady increase according to the size of the boat. All bilge suction lines should terminate in a strum box or gauze which has an effective area of at least three times the cross-sectional area of the pipe. This allows for the pump still to operate even though the suction is partially blocked by foreign matter.

There should be no foreign matter in the bilges of a well maintained boat, but there may always be some debris floating about. Even if it is not solid matter, it may be oil and this can cause trouble if pumped overboard. Pumping oil into the sea is prohibited in many coastal areas and therefore it may be necessary to pump oily bilge water ashore. The moral is not to get oil into the bilges in the first place.

Stricter laws on pollution also make it illegal to discharge toilets overboard in many parts of the world, particularly in harbours. This is not a serious problem for fishing boats at present, but it is likely to be in the future and more attention will have to be given to toilet installations. The common toilet which is flushed by sea water and discharges overboard will no longer be acceptable, nor will the bucket which is used on many small boats.

The alternatives available are special toilets which treat the sewage before it is pumped overboard, chemical toilets, or a holding tank. The toilets which treat the sewage are electrically operated and require a sea water supply. It is possible that this type may not be acceptable when stricter pollution laws are introduced.

Chemical toilets, in which a special liquid put into the toilet pan treats the sewage, have the benefit of simplicity, but because the pan gradually fills, the contents may slop over the side if the boat rolls or pitches heavily. A modern type uses a built in holding tank and recirculates the liquid by means of an electric pump when the toilet is flushed. The same pump can be used to discharge the liquid overboard either when well out at sea or into a holding tank ashore.

A holding tank on board simply utilizes a toilet flushed in the normal way with sea water by means of a hand or an electric pump, and then the discharge is led to the holding tank where the sewage is contained until it can be pumped ashore. Obviously the tank must be of adequate size to suit the number of crew and the duration of the voyage, and it is usually a steel tank on wooden boats or a tank built into the double bottom on steel or GRP boats. It must be very carefully constructed to avoid leaks and it should not be directly adjacent to a fresh water tank. The pumping out fitting is usually a screwed connection pipe terminating in a fitting on deck.

Whatever type of toilet is fitted, it must be carefully constructed. It is easy to dismiss the toilet as something to stow away in its own small compartment and which does not need much care and attention, but a defective system is unpleasant and can cause a leak which could sink the boat. The latter could arise where sea water is used to flush the toilet. The water is drawn from a skin fitting below the waterline and the toilet itself is often below the waterline so that any leak will introduce water into the hull.

The installation should be to the same high standards as the engine cooling system. Plastic piping is acceptable and can make the installation much simpler, but this piping must be of the reinforced type and should be secured at each end by double stainless steel worm drive clips. Plated clips will corrode very rapidly.

Seacocks should be fitted on both the inlet and the discharge pipe. A non-return valve can usefully be fitted on the discharge as an added precaution against intake of sea water. Seacocks will rapidly cease to function if not cared for. A drop of oil on the spindle and working the valve once a week could prevent disaster in the event of the pipe failing at sea. The valves must be placed in an accessible position so that they can be found easily in an emergency.

The toilet facilities on fishing boats have been treated very casually in the past, but this situation will change as crews demand better conditions on board and legislation is introduced to reinforce them. The same applies to the fresh water system. A hand pump drawing direct from the fresh water tank will no longer be acceptable, and hot and cold running water will be required.

There is no difficulty in providing for this amenity but it adds to the complication of the boat. Fresh water is contained in a tank, usually of steel, and most of the remarks about fuel tanks are applicable to the fresh water tank except that a sump and drain cock are not necessary. It is normal to coat the inside of the tank with a cement wash or a special preparation. The size of the tank should be a balance between having sufficient water for the duration of one or more trips, but not so large that the water is not changed at frequent intervals. The capacity will frequently be dictated by the space available for the tank.

Flexible tanks of a special rubber are a modern substitute for steel fresh water tanks. These can be obtained in a variety of sizes and are easily installed in whatever spaces are available. Filling and outlet pipes must be flexible to accommodate the movement of the tank as it is filled and emptied. Whatever tanks are used it is advisable to divide

74

the water capacity between at least two tanks so if one becomes contaminated there will still be some water remaining.

A hand pump can be used to draw water from the tank, but modern electric pumps are simple to install, require little maintenance and provide running water automatically when the tap is opened. These automatic pumps are essential where a hot water system is fitted.

Water can be heated by four methods: gas heating, electric heating, oil heating and by using the waste heat from the engine. The choice between the first three will depend largely on the system used for cooking and heating, and it is logical to use the same type of power for each. The waste heat from the engine can be used for both water heating and heating the accommodation, but not for cooking.

The fresh water cooling flow from the engine is passed through a calorifier which is simply a heat exchanger in which the fresh water for washing and heating radiators flows. A well insulated storage tank is installed in the system, normally combined with the calorifier, and the fresh water pumping system provides the pressure.

The whole system is rather like the central heating system in a house and by keeping the engine cooling system and the domestic system separate there is less chance of leaks putting the engine out of action.

Electrical and oil heating systems are very similar in as much as they have a boiler which supplies the hot water which is then distributed by a pump. Both oil and electricity could be used for cooking in stoves designed for the purpose, but these are usually restricted to the larger boats referred to in this book. Electricity for cooking and heating demands a large generator. Oil is convenient as it uses the same fuel as the engine, but boilers and cooking stoves are large and complex and need their own exhausts.

Gas contained in rechargeable cylinders is probably one of the most widely used fuels for heating and cooking on small fishing boats. The various units such as water heaters, cookers and cabin heaters are small and easy to install. They are independent of the engine so that they can be used in harbour and they are clean in use. The gas itself is very dangerous, being highly explosive, so great care must be taken that all the joints are leakproof. The gas cylinders themselves are always stowed on deck so that any leakage of gas is quickly dispersed.

Gas leaking inside the hull will find its way down into the bilges where it can form an explosive mixture with air, which a spark will ignite. Boats fitted with gas appliances must be fitted with a gas detector and alarm to give warning of any dangerous build up. A fan draws air from the bilges so that the gas can be removed before any electric appliances are switched on or the engine started.

Cabin heaters of any type must be securely fastened so that they cannot move when the boat is at sea. Otherwise there is a serious risk of fire. Warm air heating is probably the best method, particularly if the heating tubes and the fan which blows the air over them can be contained in the engine compartment. This keeps all the machinery together so that it is more likely to be serviced regularly and reduces the length of the piping runs.

The warm air can be ducted through the boat by means of flexible tubing, making for a simple installation. This air not only keeps the accommodation and wheelhouse warm, but also keeps it dry, very necessary both for comfort and for keeping rot and corrosion at bay.

A fishing boat at sea has to be self-contained. All the services required on board have to be provided from the boat's own resources. The resulting complications can lead to unreliability unless the installations have been carefully thought out at the start. The systems should be as simple as possible within the requirements of efficiency and comfort. As many services as possible should be combined, so that as much as possible is run by the same type of power.

Fishermen are now demanding all the conveniences of home on board their craft. These can be provided, but at a price, both in terms of cost and complication. Much of the development of services has come from the yachting world where comfort has high priority. Comfort has its place on fishing boats and crews are likely to be more efficient on a comfortable boat.

CHAPTER 6

Stern Gear

Having an engine of the power to give the required performance is one thing. Transmitting the power of the engine into usable thrust to drive the boat along is another and it is only by careful attention to the many parameters which affect propeller performance that the desired results will be achieved. Even so it will be a compromise because, generally, the propulsion system can only be designed to give optimum performance under one particular set of conditions.

The standard propulsion system utilizes a gearbox coupled directly to the engine. This in turn may be coupled to a reduction gear, but it is now common for the reduction gear to be incorporated in the gearbox giving a more compact unit. The drive from the gearbox or reduction gearbox is taken directly, by shaft, to the propeller.

Modern gearboxes incorporate the selection of neutral, ahead and astern as well as the reduction gear, and these are combined in an enclosed unit which requires little maintenance. The design of gearboxes varies but in general they have two plate clutches which are operated hydraulically to engage either ahead or astern gear, the gears being in constant mesh. The power for the hydraulic engagement system may come from the high pressure side of the engine lubrication system, or more commonly, a separate oil pump is driven from the input shaft of the gear box which both supplies the hydraulic pressure and circulates the oil around the gearbox. The hydraulic operation of the gearchange provides ease of engagement of the gears and the clutches are self adjusting.

Because the clutch plates operate in an oil bath, wear of the plates is slow and these gearboxes will work for long periods without attention other than periodic oil checks and changes. Most gearbox failures occur through omission to maintain the level of the gearbox oil or to change it at the prescribed intervals. This can easily happen because the gearbox will give little indication that anything is wrong.

Gearboxes with a small oil capacity are often fitted with an oil cooler because the oil can become hot from the constant meshing of the gears. The first indication of impending trouble with a gearbox will normally be an increase in the temperature of the oil. Therefore an oil temperature gauge or alarm should be fitted to give warning of high temperatures or low oil level. Given warning it may be possible to maintain low engine speed to return to harbour. A device fitted to some gearboxes is the automatic engagement of ahead gear if the hydraulic control system fails, to enable the boat to return to harbour.

On most engines for small fishing boats, the gearbox is bolted directly onto the engine and relies on the engine mounting to support it. Larger engines often incorporate separate mountings for the gearbox even though it is still firmly connected to the engine. This helps to transmit the thrust of the propeller to the engine beds and thus to the structure of the boat. The bearings of the output shaft of the gearbox must be designed to take this longitudinal thrust, which can be considerable. The gearbox, link between the engine and the propeller, can be subject to very high stress should the propeller be fouled by a rope or strike a submerged object. One reason for fitting a flexible coupling between the gearbox and the propeller shaft is to cushion these stresses. When fitted solely for this purpose, it is usually of the rubber type which only allows for a very slight angular difference between the shafts but is designed to absorb the rotational stresses. Where the engine and gearbox are flexibly mounted, a flexible coupling capable of absorbing the maximum movement must be fitted. This must absorb the rotational stresses and the propeller thrust, as well as allow for angular movement between the shafts.

Whether the engine and gearbox are solidly or flexibly mounted, the engine and propeller shaft lines must be very carefully aligned. A flexible coupling in the shaft line is not a substitute for poor alignment of the shafts, because there will still be excessive pressure on the bearings which will produce rapid wear and vibration. In cases of very bad shaft alignment the constant flexing of the shaft could result in it breaking, but there would normally be adequate warning in that shaft bearings would become hot. A hot shaft bearing cannot be cured by more lubrication; the basic cause, which will normally be poor alignment, should be sought.

On a new boat or where work has been done on the shafts, the initial alignment is carried out ashore, but this should always be repeated when the boat is afloat with her normal load on board. The hull shape will alter slightly when it enters the water and it is in this condition that the shafts have to run true. The line of the propeller shaft itself cannot be altered and adjustment is done by inserting shims under the engine feet to vary the line of the crankshaft. Once properly adjusted the bolts holding down the engine must be firmly locked.

Alignment of the shafts is normally measured at the coupling flange by means of feeler gauges. Once the engine and gearbox have been secured in the correct position the flange bolts are tightened up and the nuts locked. Locking the nuts is not essential, but it is a wise precaution, and the same applies to the nuts holding the coupling flanges onto the shaft tapers.

Many fishing boats have the engine mounted aft so that the gearbox output shaft is coupled directly to the propeller shaft. Modern stern trawlers often have the engine mounted forward to obtain the maximum space in the fish hold aft, and this entails a long propeller shaft, perhaps in two or three sections. Each intermediate bearing on the shaft must be carefully aligned, starting from the fixed end, which is the propeller shaft itself.

Where a long shaft such as this is fitted, the intermediate shafts are normally of steel but the propeller shaft itself, where corrosion could be a serious problem, is made from stainless steel or Monel metal, both of which have good corrosion resistance and mechanical properties. The material from which the propeller shaft is made is a good indication of the quality of a boat. If an ordinary steel shaft has been used the shaft should have a seal at the aft end of the stern tube to reduce the risk of corrosion. When stainless steel has been used this must be of the correct type and EN 58 B is usually specified.

Where an intermediate shaft or shafts are used, the supporting bearings must be readily accessible. As they are normally under the fish hold this causes problems because simple hatches will allow water from melted ice and slurry to gather in the bearing compartment. Any hatch fitted in the bottom of the fish hold should be watertight, but these become difficult to open, and there may be quantities of ice or fish stowed on top preventing access. A better arrangement is to have the bearings at the end of the fish hold with a recess giving access from either the engine compartment or the steering compartment/store aft. These are points which should be considered during the design of the vessel. A shaft bearing which is not accessible will give trouble sooner or later. Access is not required for lubrication. This is achieved by means of a remote screw-down greaser and a pipe to lead the grease to the bearing. Access is necessary for a regular visual examination which can detect overheating or wear before it reaches serious proportions.

It is possible for a bearing to fail in spite of having been apparently well lubricated. The reason is that at some time the pipe or its connections have come apart and the grease being pumped in was going straight into the bilge instead of the bearing. The same lubrication system is frequently employed for lubricating the propeller shaft where plain metal supporting bearings are fitted. The pipes leading the grease to the bearings must be carefully sited where they will not be damaged and the connecting unions must be locked so that they will not come loose. There is usually a great deal of vibration in the area of the stern tube which will shake loose the most firmly tightened nut unless it is securely locked.

The stern tube bearings used on fishing boats fall into the following categories: the plain metal bearing and the ball or roller bearing which are lubricated by grease or oil, and the synthetic material bearing which is lubricated by water. The metal bearing is commonly used at the front of the shaft where it combines with the stern gland to provide a support for the shaft. On larger fishing boats a similar type of bearing is also used at the aft end, in which case a seal is fitted at the aft end of the shaft to prevent water and grit entering the bearings. With such a system it is permissible to use an ordinary steel shaft because it is effectively sealed off from the effects of corrosion.

The shaft which runs in ball or roller bearings will run more smoothly and is less prone to wear than that which runs on synthetic bearings, but the seals fitted at the aft end must have particular attention because no sea water must be allowed to enter the stern tube. An oil seal is fitted at the front end of the shaft and the bearings run in a bath of grease or oil. The front bearing is often of the taper type which takes the thrust from the propeller, thus relieving the engine and gearbox from these stresses. This type of stern tube is not common to fishing boats because the seals are susceptible to damage when a rope or wire is caught round the propeller. This is a frequent hazard to fishing boats more so than to other craft.

The water lubricated bearings are commonly used on small boats because they are both simple and reliable. They can be fitted to both ends of the stern tube, but normal practice is to use a metal bearing at the front of the tube and a water bearing at the aft end. The water lubricated bearing is made from moulded synthetic rubber, plastic material, or sometimes lignum vitae. This is not solid all round, but has longitudinal channels in it to allow a free flow of water through the bearing. This water flow is essential to lubricate the bearing and to wash away any grit from the bearing surfaces.

The water flow for these bearings can be collected by small scoops projecting from each side of the bearing which directs the water flowing past the hull through the bearing, or a bleed from the engine cooling water system can be fed to the bearing. This engine water bleed is essential where a water lubricated bearing is fitted inboard, but is a good idea even when the scoops are fitted. The scoops are small and are frequently found to be blocked when the boat has been afloat for some while. Marine growth can quickly build up over the scoops and these bearings will not last long if they are run dry or partially dry. The engine water supply to the bearing at least ensures that a flow is maintained whenever the engine is running.

Water lubricated bearings are particularly suitable for use in shallow water or where a boat works off a beach. They can withstand a great deal of grit in the water and yet still have a long life. When worn, replacement is fairly easy once the propeller has been removed. When synthetic rubber is used as the bearing material, it is slightly resilient and will absorb very slight misalignment of the shaft.

The stern gland at the front of the propeller shaft prevents water entering the boat *via* the shafting. It is filled with a packing material which is compressed by a sleeve around the shaft when tightened by securing bolts. The stern gland will only keep the water out if it has been packed properly and adjusted correctly. The packing used is normally a square cross-section woven rope impregnated with graphite, but some modern packings use improved synthetic materials. The packing must be of the size for which the gland was designed and should be fitted in complete circles with the joints staggered.

When properly adjusted, the gland should prevent any water from passing, but because of the possibility of overtightening the gland and causing overheating, the gland is normally adjusted so that a trickle of water comes through. It is preferable to stop the water completely because the water flow will carry with it small particles of grit which will cause wear, and the gland can easily be checked for overheating by touch. It is important for the adjusting sleeve to be tightened down evenly to prevent binding, and this is why three studs are preferable to two for the adjustment.

When newly packed the gland will need adjusting several times before the packing settles down. During this time it should be checked frequently both for leaking and overheating. Once settled down the packing should only need adjustment at infrequent intervals and if frequent adjustment is required or the flow cannot be completely stopped when the shaft is turning, wear in the stern tube bearings must be suspect. The stern gland should always be reasonably accessible and preferably not buried under the fish hold so that it can be checked without difficulty.

Consideration has to be given in the original design of the boat for the propeller shaft to be removed for examination and possible replacement of the bearings. This may be required only every two or three years, but it should not involve having to dismantle half the boat. If intermediate shafts are fitted, it may be convenient to remove one of these and draw the propeller shaft inboard, having first removed the propeller, of course.

If this is not practicable, for example when the engine is fitted close to the propeller shaft, the shaft must be drawn from aft. This means that the coupling flange must be accessible for removal and, if possible, the rudder should be constructed so that the shaft can be withdrawn without removing the rudder. If the rudder stock runs the full length of the rudder blade, this will not be possible unless the rudder is offset to one side. Alternatively, a hole can be cut in the rudder blade so that the shaft can be drawn through the hole when the rudder is placed hard over.

It may be thought unnecessary to consider all these aspects, but a great deal of money can be saved during overhauls if details such as these are worked out. The owner should be aware of such matters so that he can advise the repair yard on how the job can be done, thereby avoiding loss of time trying one way unsuccessfully.

The propeller is probably one of the most complex design problems on a boat. Owing to the many conflicting requirements involved, the propeller design will always be a compromise, but if this is directed towards the particular use to which the boat is to be put, the owner is likely to obtain the best possible results. Well designed propellers can result in an improved fuel economy, improved speed, improved pull and better performance in rough seas, but only if careful attention is paid to the problems involved. There may be some extra expense initially because the first propeller designed for the boat may not be quite right and the only way to improve performance is to fit a new propeller. The first propeller will not be completely wasted: it will have given a yardstick from which to design the second propeller and it can always be available as a spare for emergency use.

The space in which the propeller has to work is equally as important as the propeller itself, and this is decided in the original design. The propeller can only work efficiently if there is a good flow of water through and round it. Turbulent water from distorted sections of the hull or from appendages in front of the propeller will detract from its efficiency. One of the worst offenders is the deadwood directly in front of the propeller. This cannot be removed completely because it is there to give strength to the hull and to support the propeller shaft, but it can be faired at its aft end to improve the flow, particularly away from the boss.

On metal boats it is much easier to fit a thin deadwood and in some cases it is cut away altogether leaving a strut to support the propeller shaft bearing with the stern tube mounted in the hull some distance away. On GRP boats the deadwood is often narrowed above and below the propeller boss, but this can only be done if the mould is in two halves, otherwise the hull would not come out of the mould.

The size of the propeller aperture determines the diameter of the propeller which can be fitted. A restriction on the size of this aperture is imposed at the top by the need to keep the propeller well below the surface so that it

Fig 34   The balanced rudder on a small boat. The hole in the rudder allows the shaft to be withdrawn without removing the rudder. The bolted on lower rudder bearing allows for easy rudder removal.

does not suck air down and cause cavitation. At the bottom the aperture terminates in the keel extension aft which forms the lower support for the rudder. This extension could be removed and alternative means found to support the rudder, but it also forms a useful protection for the propeller in the event of grounding.

Given the space available, the diameter of the propeller will be further restricted by the need to maintain adequate clearance around the propeller. At the tips, both top and bottom, this should be at least one twelfth of the diameter of the propeller and a good clearance must be maintained between the deadwood and the propeller and the propeller and the rudder or rudder post in the fore and aft direction. These clearances can be reduced, but there will be a loss of efficiency and the plating or planking above the propeller can become worn because of the abrasive effect of grit in the water.

While in general the propeller diameter should be as large as possible, it is governed by the space available. The other major parameter which has to be decided is the pitch of the propeller, or the distance it would travel in one revolution if working in a liquid with no slip. The pitch is related to the expected speed of the boat taking into account the power available, the reduction ratio used in the gearbox and the speed of the engine. These parameters have to be assessed together to arrive at a satisfactory combination, and these in turn are related to the diameter of the propeller. The larger the diameter, the greater distance it will travel in one revolution given the same pitch.

Generally speaking, the propeller designer is looking for the largest diameter possible with a reasonably shallow pitch. Too steep a pitch will make the propeller inefficient for a displacement boat and too shallow a pitch will waste unnecessary power in friction. The engine speed on modern high speed diesels will be too fast for a direct drive on fishing boats and therefore a reduction gear is necessary. A reduction of up to 5:1 may be used to allow for the good thrust characteristics of a large diameter slow turning propeller.

The task of the propeller designer is made more difficult on fishing boats because not only does the propeller have to provide a satisfactory full speed, but also a good thrust at lower speeds for towing a trawl. The more thrust available at lower speeds, the larger the trawl which can be towed, but this should not be achieved at the expense of a very inefficient cruising speed.

One method to increase the thrust of a propeller is to place it in a nozzle. For the best results, propeller and nozzle have to be carefully matched, and several firms market propeller and nozzle sets. The nozzle is aerofoil in cross-section and tapers slightly towards the stern, thus accelerating the flow of water through it. Four bladed propellers are commonly used and these have squared tips to give a close working tolerance with the nozzle. Thrust can be increased by as much as 20% by the use of a nozzle, but there is likely to be a slight loss of efficiency in top speed because of the added resistance of the nozzle. These nozzles are now becoming available for boats as small as 40 feet long and are a common fitment on steel fishing boats.

Many marine engine builders have much experience in selecting the right propeller for the engine. They know that the engine they supply will only do its job satisfactorily and produce the right speed and towing characteristics if the right propeller and reduction gears are fitted. They often have an expert on their staff who studies the results of all the engine installations carried out, and from this experience is able to advise the correct equipment for a particular boat.

While these experts can do a good job, and it is certainly important to get advice from an expert when it comes to propeller design, they cannot achieve the impossible. With a fixed blade propeller they are trying to make it do two jobs, namely efficient free running speed and

Fig 35   A propeller nozzle fitted to a boat. The lumps on the outside of the nozzle are anodes to reduce the electrolytic corrosion between the steel nozzle and the bronze propeller.

good towing at lower speeds. The result must be a compromise. Better results can be achieved by using a controllable pitch propeller, and while this may give greater efficiency there are also disadvantages, and it has not been adopted universally for fishing boats.

With a controllable pitch propeller, the angle of the propeller blades can be altered in relation to the fixed propeller boss, so allowing the pitch of the propeller to be varied. If full speed is required when free running, the blades are set near maximum pitch, but for towing when the load is heavier and the boat will not move so far forward with each propeller revolution, a smaller pitch is set.

By being able to select the pitch at will, one can adjust the propeller to suit any particular circumstances so that the engine is always running at maximum efficiency. If the bottom of the boat is dirty and causing added resistance, then a slightly smaller pitch will still keep the engine running at its proper speed and not overload it. The same applies in a head sea when the increased resistance of the waves can be compensated for.

Fig 36 A fixed propeller on a steel-hulled vessel. The simple balanced rudder is stiffened by the horizontal bars.

Fig 37 A three bladed controllable pitch propeller. Note the larger hub required.

The controllable pitch propeller also eliminates the need for an ahead and astern gearbox because the pitch can be brought to zero or reversed to give neutral or astern movement. Control is very precise and smooth and there is no doubt that the use of these propellers can increase engine life, but at some cost. If these propellers offer so much, why have they not been more widely adopted?

There are several disadvantages with the controllable pitch propeller and the fisherman must weigh these against the advantages. Cost is one of the main factors; the cost of the propeller together with its operating mechanism is comparable to that of a normal gearbox and shaft installation. One still requires a clutch and a reduction gear fitted to the engine, so the overall cost will be considerably higher. This has to be offset against possible savings in fuel consumption and engine maintenance.

Although the controllable pitch propeller will be more efficient than the fixed blade propeller, the larger boss required to house the actuating mechanism and support the blades creates more resistance. Because the blades can only be shaped for one particular speed they will be less efficient at other speeds. Probably the greatest disadvantage to controllable pitch propellers is the risk of damage from trawl wires or submerged objects. Many fishermen fear that damage to a propeller could put their boat out of commission for long periods. It would inevitably involve slipping the boat.

Experience has shown that damage is not a severe problem and in most cases of striking an object the damage is confined to the outer part of the blade. A wire around the propeller boss will render the propeller inoperative as it will a conventional propeller, but it is unlikely to damage the mechanism. The clutch fitted into the drive system enables the propeller to be stopped completely if there is a danger of entanglement with a wire.

For many fishermen, lack of confidence in the controllable pitch propeller is largely fear of the unknown. Because service facilities for these units are not readily available in many areas the fisherman is unlikely to adopt such a unit in the same way that he looks for the ready availability of engine spares. Where these propellers have been adopted for fishing such as in Sweden, the change has been almost universal and the propellers have operated very successfully. It should be added that controllable pitch propellers are not generally suitable for boats under 40 feet in length.

Most fishing boats are fitted with a rope guard which covers the gap between the end of the stern tube and the propeller boss. This gap is the usual place for ropes to jamb into if they foul the propeller, and once in they are extremely difficult to remove, particularly synthetic ropes which tend to melt in to the groove through friction. The rope guard is simply a metal ring which fits closely over this gap and it should be maintained in good condition if trouble is to be avoided.

Larger guards are sometimes fitted right around the propeller. They may help to stop a rope or wire becoming entangled with the propeller, but once in, the rope will be much more difficult to remove. The main purpose of these guards is to protect the propeller when boats are working in ice.

One of the main objections to using twin screws on fishing boats is the increased possibility of the propeller fouling the fishing gear. When a wing engine is fitted, it is placed on the side away from which the gear is worked. The installation of the shaft and gear is very similar to that of a single screw except that there is no stern tube as such, the shaft being supported at the point where it leaves the hull and by a bearing in the shaft bracket which supports the propeller. The remainder of the shaft is exposed, although in some craft a tube is fitted to enclose the shaft and this provides additional support for the propeller bracket.

Ropes or wires around the propeller are a relatively common occurrence with fishing boats. This is due to the methods of operating fishing gear. A simple device, if designed into the hull before construction begins, will not prevent the ropes fouling the propeller, but it will make the task of clearing them easier. This device is a wide tube fitted immediately above the propeller and terminating in a watertight hatch on deck. When the hatch is opened there is access to the propeller with a boathook or a knife on a pole.

Such a tube must be watertight and is difficult to construct on a wooden boat. It is comparatively easy to fit to a steel or a GRP boat, but the deck hatch must be kept not only watertight, but airtight, otherwise air entering the tube will cause cavitation at the propeller. Ideally, the tube should be sealed at the lower end with a plug, maintaining the continuity of the hull shape above the propeller so that there is no interference with the water flow in this area.

All work connected with the propeller and its fittings needs to be carried out with care and great attention to detail. All nuts should be locked because when the boat is at sea little can be done if any faults develop, except to obtain a tow. The same need for care applies to the rudder. The rudder is expected to work for year after year with little or no attention. The fact that it usually does is due to the method of original construction.

While a boat's machinery in general is maintained, the steering gear on fishing boats invariably suffers from neglect. Often the first time it is noticed that something is wrong is when the steering fails, yet if the regular examinations had been carried out the defects would have been noticed and remedied long before they became serious. Wear on the steering is gradual, but it takes place steadily and like everything else on the boat it must have its share of regular maintenance.

On modern fishing boats, the rudder fitted is usually of the balanced type where part of the blade is forward of the pivot. By using a balanced rudder the load on the blade is partially equalised thus reducing the power needed to turn the rudder. In addition, the balanced rudder has a better steering effect because it is operating in a larger area of the propeller thrust and so more of this is deflected to the side than with an unbalanced rudder.

The unbalanced rudder is normally hinged to a rudder post which completes the propeller aperture aft of the propeller. This provides a stronger hull when wood is the building material, but this is easily compensated for with modern building methods.

Rudder blades can be constructed from wood, steel or GRP. Wooden blades have steel reinforcing which will normally also form the hinges. These blades are satisfactory until corrosion attacks the steel or rot affects the timber, but their thickness, which is necessary for strength, reduces efficiency. Steel is the most commonly used material for rudder blades and these are usually of the single plate type with stiffening, which is both cheap and effective.

GRP is being used as a corrosion resistant material for rudders and it is often moulded over a steel frame for added strength. Part or all of the rudder stock should be moulded in to allow for the rudder to be hung. A

Fig 38 The aft end of a GRP fishing boat. The vertical tube gives access from the deck to the propeller for clearing any ropes or nets which have fouled it.

moulded rudder can be shaped to an aerofoil section which offers less resistance and can be turned to a greater angle before stalling. The same shape can be achieved with a double plate steel rudder, but this is an expensive fabrication.

The rudder is mounted on a stock, which in turn is supported by two or three bearings. The bottom bearing is almost invariably carried in the keel extension which passes under the propeller, and the top bearing is usually combined with the gland fitted at the top of the rudder stock to prevent water entering the hull. Exceptions are where the rudder is hung from the transom, when a system of pintles and gudgeons is used with probably a bottom support from the keel extension, and when the rudder stock extends above deck level so that no gland is required.

The position of the third bearing will vary with the design of the boat. It is only required when the stock is long or is of small diameter in relation to its length, when it will deflect if it is not supported. Modern rudder stocks are usually of stainless steel or Monel metal to reduce corrosion, particularly on the bearing surfaces.

It should be simple to remove the rudder and stock both for examination of the bearings and possibly to simplify removal of the propeller shaft. Because there is rarely the depth available on a slipway for the rudder and stock to be withdrawn in one piece, there is usually a joining flange inserted in the stock just above the rudder. By freeing this flange and raising the stock, the rudder can be lifted out of the bottom bearing.

All rudder bearings should be of a replaceable type so that worn bearings can be easily removed. So often bearings are simply formed in the hull structure so that when wear takes place, major building up and machining has to be done on the hull. This is more likely with the lower rudder bearing, where wear can be very rapid if the boat takes the bottom or operates in water where silt is present. This bearing should always be fitted with a drain so that water and grit do not lie in the bearing but are washed through.

When designing the rudder, provision should be made for one of the bearings to take the weight of the rudder, and also to prevent the rudder lifting when the stern of the boat is rising and falling in a seaway. The keel bearing usually carries the weight of the rudder and the middle bearing is often fitted for the prime purpose of preventing the rudder lifting. In incorporating all these provisions, thought must always be given to dismantling the rudder for overhaul. This will probably only be done regularly if it is easy.

The gland fitted to prevent water from entering the hull is very similar to that used on the stern gland. It must be made reasonably accessible so that it receives the attention it deserves. The bearing incorporated with the gland is often fitted with a greaser to lubricate it, and in general all the remarks applicable to the stern gland apply to the rudder gland, except that it is unlikely to overheat if tightened too much, but the steering will become stiff.

Attached to the rudder stock above the gland is the quadrant or tiller. There are several methods of turning this, including rod and chain, wire and pulley, rod and gears, push pull cable and hydraulic systems. Rod and chain was a very popular system, with the rods running in channels on each side of the boat and chains connecting these to the wheel at one end and the quadrant at the other. It works well if properly installed and maintained, but it requires more physical effort in steering and the chains wear quickly, particularly at the quadrant and around the pulleys.

Wire and pulley is a similar system, the rods and chains being substituted by a continuous wire with turns around a drum attached to the steering wheel. It can work well provided that the wire is kept properly tensioned and a second steering wheel can be incorporated without too much difficulty, although both have to turn at the same time. The pulleys in the system come under considerable strain and must be bolted in position, never screwed. Great care must be taken to provide a straight lead for the wires between the pulleys, otherwise rapid wear will take place.

The wires and pulleys of this system must be protected against any loose gear which might become entangled and foul them. For this reason they should not run through gear lockers unprotected nor should the system of rods and gears. This latter system is less prone to being jammed because only the rods are turning and the gears are normally fully enclosed. The rod and gear method employs a direct shafting between the wheel and the rudder tiller with the gearboxes being used where a change of direction is required. It is reliable, but also expensive. A second steering position can be incorporated.

For smaller boats the push-pull cable is a common fitment because it is relatively cheap and easy to install. A thick cable moves within a heavy outer casing and transmits the wheel movements *via* a rack and pinion to the tiller. Installation is simple because the cable can be bent around curves, and as the outer cable does not move there is no risk of jamming. The inner cable is sealed and lubricated so that wear is minimized.

A second steering position can be added but this can add to complications. Also a double cable can be installed so that when one is pushing the other is pulling. This provides easier steering, particularly when the wheel is hard over.

Hydraulic steering is being used almost exclusively on larger fishing boats and is finding greater favour on smaller boats despite its high initial cost. It provides a reliable steering system with the only moving parts being at the wheel and at the tiller arm, the connection between being by means of rigid or flexible hydraulic pipes. These pipes must be secured to prevent any movement and they must be protected against damage, particularly where they pass through the fish hold.

The wheel turns a simple hydraulic pump which may be of the rotary or piston type. This forces oil along the delivery pipe, which in turn actuates the piston which moves the tiller. This piston works in a double acting cylinder so that either pipe can act as the delivery pipe, depending on which way the wheel is turned.

An alternative type of hydraulic steering utilizes what is in effect a hydraulic motor mounted directly onto the rudder stock. Oil under pressure forced into the circular cylinder turns the rudder stock, one benefit being that equal force is exerted irrespective of the angle of the rudder. With other types of steering where a tiller is pulled to and fro, maximum steering force is exerted when the rudder is amidships, and

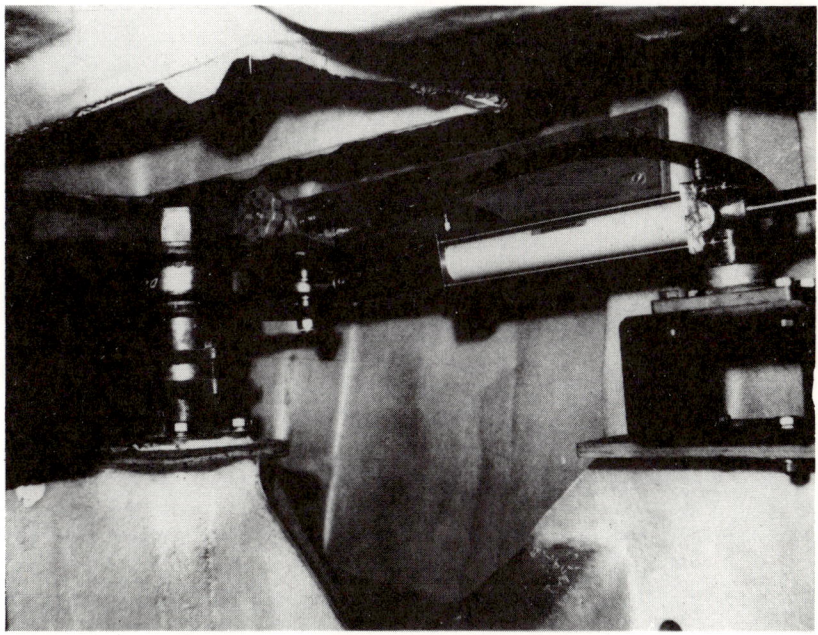

Fig 39 Single arm hydraulic steering gear on a GRP fishing boat. The valve close to the rudder stock is a bypass so that hand steering can be used in the event of any failure in the hydraulic system.

it gradually decreases the further the rudder is turned, just when it ought to be increasing. This is due to the geometry of the steering, allowing that the turning lever is at a maximum when the rudder is amidships.

Some fishermen prefer this type of steering as it gives them 'feel' and they can judge how much helm is on by the force needed to turn the wheel. This is certainly the case where a rudder is hinged at its forward end, but is less so with a balanced rudder. One of the criticisms made at hydraulic steering is that the steering feels 'dead' largely because the wheel stays where it is left and does not return to amidships of its own accord. This can be an advantage when hauling or shooting gear, but it can make the boat less easy to steer.

On the fishing boats covered by this book it should be possible to arrange the steering system so that it can be operated by hand with no servo-assistance required. This requires careful design of the whole system to make it as free as possible. In particular the shape and balance of the rudder are of great importance. When servo-assistance is fitted, the steering can be very light indeed. This can give easy control, but the added complication and expense is not always justified.

Servo-assisted steering demands a hydraulic pump which is usually belt driven from the main engine or electrically driven. This supplies the oil pressure to the tiller actuating piston or motor under the control of instructions from the wheel. Servo-assisted steering is essential when an auto-pilot is fitted.

Like the propeller, not much can be done if the rudder fails at sea. This is a good reason for maintaining it in good condition. Rudder failure can only be overcome if the boat is fitted with twin engines, and then only if the rudder has not jammed in the 'hard-over' position. Failure of the operating mechanism can be overcome by fitting a hand tiller, which usually mounts on a square fitted on the top of the rudder stock with access through a deck plug. The hand tiller will only work if the normal steering system is disconnected and this should be provided for in the design of the system. All nuts and bolts in the steering system should be securely locked.

Provided the whole of the stern gear is checked at annual overhauls it should give satisfactory performance. The increasing number of failures in steering gear arises because fishermen have ignored the warning signal when the boat is afloat, increased vibration must always be suspect. When the boat is hauled out it is a simple matter to give the stern gear a visual check and to check for wear, and no chances should be taken if any wear is found.

CHAPTER 7

Safety Equipment

The successful operation of almost every part of a boat contributes towards the safety of that boat in some way, and the best overall approach to safety is to maintain the craft to a standard where no part of it fails. The majority of fishing boats which get into trouble can trace the cause of the disaster to some part which has failed.

The failure can be that of a minor item. For example, the compass light could fail on a dark stormy night. During the time a torch was being found the helmsman could become disorientated and allow the boat to come onto a dangerous heading. Also, failures can be cumulative. Consider, for instance, a steering wire may break in moderate sea conditions. In itself, this would not be too serious as the equipment to make a temporary repair may be on board. However, in breaking, the steering wire could fall across the battery terminals, causing a short circuit which in turn might start a fire. It may seem unlikely to have to abandon ship because of a fire which started because of a steering failure, but it has happened and there are reports of many similar types of accidents.

The essential point is that having safety equipment on board does not absolve the owner or skipper from maintaining his boat properly. The best insurance of all against disaster is to have a well maintained boat. The safety equipment is only there to help save life should matters get out of control.

In recent years there has been a marked increase in the regulations stipulating the safety equipment a fishing boat should carry. Most of these are applicable to fishing boats of particular nations and stem from a perhaps over-zealous approach to the increasing number of fishing boat casualties.

Safety regulations are gradually being applied to smaller fishing boats, where perhaps they should have started. One or two men can drown without too much publicity, but governments must be seen to be doing something if twenty men drown. Most of these safety regulations dictate the safety equipment which fishing boats should carry, and these will eventually be combined in a universal set of safety rules produced by IMCO when all the many countries concerned can agree.

In the meantime, there are sensible precautions for a fisherman to take, one being to have the means to abandon ship if the fishing boat sinks, catches fire, or runs ashore. Abandoning ship is to be considered as a last resort because rescuers will find it much easier to find the vessel itself than to find individuals.

For small fishing boats the inflatable liferaft is the obvious answer within the limits of present technology. It has no means of propulsion, but this can be of benefit if it has been possible to give distress signals, because it is preferable to stay close to the position indicated. A liferaft will be blown about by the wind, but a sea anchor streamed to windward will reduce the drift.

The liferaft is carried inside a valise or GRP container to protect it from the elements. The instructions say make the painter line fast and simply toss the raft overboard. Anyone who has tried to carry a raft weighing 100 lb (50 kilos) or more on the deck of a tossing boat will appreciate the difficulties and it is as well to install a better means of launching. The position where the raft is stowed will vary from boat to boat, but on top of the accommodation or the wheelhouse are preferred. The raft should be kept away from the working deck where it is likely to be damaged and it should also be kept away from the heat, such as the funnel or exhaust.

A liferaft mounted on the wheelhouse top can simply be rolled overboard. It should clear the bulwarks if the roll is timed carefully, but it must not foul up on the gallows or other projection. Remember that one of the crew will have to go onto the wheelhouse top to release the raft, so some handholds must be provided.

On larger boats, the gap between the deckhouse and the bulwark can be bridged by a light metal ramp. This is included as part of the cradle which supports the liferaft. When the securing strap is slipped the ramp automatically falls down and forms a track for the raft to roll into the sea.

This system only allows the raft to be launched on one side of the boat, which is not ideal, but is better than just having both rafts stowed on top of the deckhouse with no easy means of getting them into the water. A similar fitting could be used to launch the raft astern, but the current tendency is for the stern of the boat to be used for fishing purposes. Nothing is perfect when dealing with emergencies and what might work for one situation may be unsuitable in another.

A liferaft would normally be launched to leeward both to give shelter when boarding the raft and to allow the raft to drift away when cast off. This would be the situation in rough weather, but if the crew were abandoning ship because it was on fire, then it might be better to take to the raft on the windward side because of the flames blowing down to

Fig 40 Liferafts stowed so that they could be difficult to launch in an emergency.

leeward. When deciding on a place to stow the raft, consider how and when it might have to be used. Imagine using it on a dark and stormy night and give the position of the liferaft slightly higher priority than it might otherwise have.

The liferaft painter should be made fast on a strong point close by the stowage. Do not pull out any more painter; there is a special seal fitted to prevent water working its way up the painter and into the container. The liferaft must be serviced at least once a year. Only if this is done will it be certain that it will work properly when required.

Most countries have some form of approval standard for liferafts which means that approved rafts have been thoroughly tested. It is sensible to buy rafts which carry this approval, but beware of clever advertising. Some liferaft manufacturers claim that the material from which the rafts are made has been approved. There is a great deal of difference between this and saying that the raft itself is approved. This is not to say that non-approved rafts are unsatisfactory. Indeed there are many innovative designs being marketed, but bear in mind that when it is necessary to use a liferaft, there is no second chance, so it is best to make sure that the best available is carried.

Fig 41 A well conceived liferaft stowage. The vertical H falls down when the raft is released making a ramp to allow the raft to roll overboard.

On some fishing vessels an inflatable boat is carried both as a tender and as part of the lifesaving equipment. This boat is carried inflated ready for use and, as such, must be carefully protected from chafing. Any movement, such as the vessel moving in a seaway, will cause the inflatable boat to move and this will chafe the fabric of the boat if there are any sharp objects in contact with it. These boats are usually fitted with an outboard motor, which while not essential for lifesaving, might just as well be kept in good order so that it will work when required and save the expense of an overhaul. The engines are always vulnerable to corrosion and damp, and a regular spray with a silicone grease aerosol will help to keep corrosion at bay.

In many areas it is the practice to carry a dory or similar small boat for emergencies. These should be fitted with integral buoyancy so that they will still float if flooded, and some form of cover is desirable to protect men from exposure. While not so effective as the inflatables, these craft are better than nothing, but legislation is likely to make them obsolete.

Lifesaving equipment will stand idle for long periods, generally without any care and attention, yet is expected to work perfectly when required. It will normally do this if it has been stowed carefully. The manufacturers make the equipment as reliable as possible, but it is the responsibility of the crew to stow the equipment where it will not come to harm and where it will be readily available in an emergency. This applies particularly to

Fig 42   Lifesaving equipment must be maintained in good condition. Someone's life might depend on this lifebuoy one day.

distress flares, which may be the only means of summoning assistance.

Flares, whether of the smoke, parachute or hand-held type, must be kept dry. It is best to make a special rack for them so that they do not roll around in a locker or drawer with other equipment. When needed, they must be conveniently to hand. Most flares have an average life of three years, varying between two and four. This information is rarely contained on the flare itself and much depends on the view of the Authority making the safety rules. A date is stamped on the flare, but to add to the confusion this may be either the date of manufacture or the date the flare is reckoned to be expired.

Different makes of flare and different types of flare have different methods of firing so these must be checked. It is too late to start reading instructions on a dark stormy night (assuming that there is a light to do it by). Do not be misled by exaggerated claims regarding the distance at which flares may be seen. These are usually based on someone watching for a pinpoint of light and knowing where to look. Ten miles is about the maximum any flare will be seen, and then only on a clear night.

Most safety rules specify the minimum number of hand flares, smoke flares and parachute flares a boat must carry. More can be carried and in this case they should be parachute flares, as these are the only ones which are really effective. Smoke flares only last for a short time, can only be seen during the day, and the smoke disperses quickly if there is much wind. Hand flares are useful to indicate your position to a rescue vessel when it is seen approaching, but for calling for help, night or day, the parachute flare is best.

The approved types of lifejacket which are required to be carried on most types of fishing boats are practically useless for any purpose other than keeping a man afloat. For a lifejacket to be of any use, it must be worn when entering the water. The approved types of lifejacket are large and cumbersome because they rely entirely on foam or kapok buoyancy to keep afloat. This makes it very difficult to do any useful work in them, which means the average fisherman will not be wearing it at the time of an emergency.

These lifejackets were designed so that a passenger on a ship could put one on satisfactorily and know that he or she would be kept afloat, face up, even when unconscious. They were never designed to work in, and the fisherman needs something in which he can both work and move about. Imagine trying to launch a liferaft wearing one of the approved lifejackets.

A lifejacket should be worn if the sea is really rough or if the crew have to work on deck in heavy seas. The more popular lifejacket is the inflatable or semi-inflatable type which is comfortable to wear, but does rely entirely on the wearer either blowing it up by mouth or operating a toggle to allow gas from a cylinder to inflate the air chamber. Of course this cannot be done if the wearer is unconscious.

Lifejackets of the inflatable type do require maintenance if they are to keep working efficiently. An annual overhaul is recommended, and they will not stand up very long to constant wear. Lifejackets should only be considered as wear for emergency situations. The individual can decide whether to wear one or the skipper can decide for him. Boats have to carry the approved type but there is no reason why a more practical design should not be carried as well. It will cost more, but when lives are at stake cost should not be a criterion.

Keeping afloat is only part of the problem. Much of the world's fishing is carried out in cold climates, where the low sea temperature can mean that survival time in the water can be measured in minutes rather than hours. Many special suits have been devised to cope with this exposure problem, some of them designed for working in, others are donned when abandoning ship. Most of these contain some form of buoyancy as well, so that they are in effect a self-contained unit. For boats regularly working in cold areas there is much to be said for such suits, but they are expensive. It is for the individual to decide on his priorities.

Lifebuoys are also for supporting people in the water and they are mandatory equipment for many types of boats. Their use is primarily to throw to someone who has fallen overboard, both to provide support until he can be rescued and to mark the spot where he is. This latter use is particularly important at night. In most boats it is necessary to have at least one lifebuoy with an automatic light fitted.

The standard ring lifebuoy, now usually made from foam filled plastic, is satisfactory for support and visibility, but almost impossible to throw far so that by the time it is launched, the man in the water will be some distance away if the boat is under way. An alternative worth considering is an inflatable lifebuoy which is contained in an easy to throw ball. This has no light so it is not much help at night.

One lifebuoy is usually required to have a line on it, but this does not help much because it is difficult to throw the buoy far. There are rescue sticks on the market where a line is coiled tightly round the handle of a small float. When thrown the line becomes uncoiled, and these rescue sticks can be thrown some distance. It is reassuring for someone in the water to be connected to the boat by line, but this is something for daytime use unless a searchlight is available.

There is no complete and simple answer to the man overboard problem, except to keep the bulwarks at a good height to make going over more difficult. While considering this subject, it is advisable to consider how to get the man back on board. Some form of ladder is essential, either for the man to climb up on his own, or for someone to go down to help him.

A ladder over the side is difficult to climb, so consider hanging one from a derrick if one is kept rigged at sea. This could be raised or lowered by a winch, and with one man already on the ladder it would be much easier to get hold of the man in the water and lift him rather than try and haul him up the side. Much will depend on the individual boat and its layout, so this must be carefully considered.

One way of avoiding going overboard is to use safety harnesses. These are worn around the body and a line with a large carbine hook is secured to a strong point. One of the main objections to using safety harnesses is that the line restricts free movement, which in itself could be dangerous when working gear. Ideally the line should be kept short enough to prevent the man going overboard, but being towed alongside can be more dangerous than falling clear. At speeds of over 8 knots there is a risk of injury from the harness if anyone falls into the water and the line jerks tight.

Like all safety equipment, the safety harness is far from perfect, but it could provide extra safety in certain circumstances. One particular case in point is the single handed fisherman where there is no one to pick him up if he falls overboard. Lifebuoys are not much use to him, but a safety harness would give him a chance. Alternatively, it could be preferable to wear a lifejacket so that he has some form of buoyancy if he goes overboard, and small packs of flares can be obtained to carry in the pocket which would give him some means of indicating his plight.

Fishing is a risky occupation and there is no means of completely eliminating the risks. As far as possible, accidents should be prevented, but remedial measures should be available. This applies particularly to fire, which is not a risk peculiar to fishing boats, but which nevertheless is a frightening occurrence at sea.

The fire risk areas in a fishing boat are the engine compartment, the wheelhouse, the accommodation and the galley. In the engine compartment, fire can result from an overheating engine or hot exhaust, a fuel leak, an electrical short circuit or, if a mechanical drive to the winch is fitted, overheating of the driving belts. Whatever the cause of an engine compartment fire, the main danger will be from the fuel which, if added to the fire, will make it very difficult to extinguish and could lead to an explosion. Therefore much attention should be given to the careful installation of the fuel system.

The wheelhouse is at risk partly because of the possibility of fire from a short circuit in the electronic equipment and partly from smoking. Smoking is also the major risk in the accommodation and probably results in more fires on board fishing boats than all the other causes combined. Tired crews falling asleep while smoking may easily cause a fire.

The heat or flames from the stove are the risk in the galley. With the boat movement there is always the risk of oil or cooking fat being spilt. Electrical fires may occur in any part of the boat where there is wiring or fittings (a good reason for keeping this in good order). The fishhold and gear compartment are low fire risk areas.

In order to deal with a fire on board it is essential to detect it in its early stages and to have the means close at hand to deal with it. Seconds count, because once a fire has a firm hold it becomes increasingly difficult to extinguish with the crew untrained in fire-fighting and the limited space to work in.

The engine compartments on most fishing boats are unattended. The first warning of fire may be a hot floor in the wheelhouse, or the engine stopping. Because the fire is contained in a closed compartment it is best dealt with by flooding the compartment with an inert gas which will exclude the oxygen which the fire needs to sustain it. It must be possible to shut off all air intakes to the compartment and any ventilating fans must be switched off.

It is possible to fit a device which will give warning of a fire in the engine compartment. This detects an abnormally high temperature and sounds an alarm in the wheelhouse. The gas cylinders which contain the inert gas (usually carbon dioxide) can be operated by remote control, which is often located in the wheelhouse. It is possible to omit the human link in this chain and have the whole system automatic, but this does not allow for the fact that there might be someone in the engine compartment, or for closing the air intakes.

Similar systems use a fire extinguishing fluid such as BCF or freon, both inert gases which are sprayed around the compartment. Alternatively, a fine water spray could be used, but this, while extinguishing the fire, could cause considerable damage to the electrical installation, and may prevent use of the engine when the fire is out. Do not be in too much of a hurry to open up the compartment once the extinguishers have been operated. The hot parts will take time to cool and a sudden inrush of oxygen could start the fire again, and there may not be a second charge in the gas cylinders.

An engine compartment fire could cause considerable heat and current legislation requires bulkheads at each end of the engine compartment which are reasonably fireproof. On wooden boats, steel bulkheads are fitted and on GRP boats special fireproof resins are used. Steel boats, of course, present no problem.

In addition to a fixed extinguishing system at least one hand extinguisher in the engine compartment should be available to deal with small fires if they are found early. The extinguishing fluid used should be suitable for use on oil fires and should be safe to deal with electrical fires if the voltage used exceeds 32 volts. Foam, while suitable for use on oil fires, does not meet the latter requirement. Therefore one of the modern extinguishing liquids such as BCF is preferable. These fluids can be dangerous to the operator in a confined space, so special care should be taken to avoid being overcome by the fumes.

Extinguishing powders are excellent for dealing with small fires, being relatively harmless to the operator. On boats, where there is continuing vibration, the powder tends to settle and harden, but some powders have a special ingredient to prevent this. These powder extinguishers are generally lighter than their liquid equivalent, an important factor where the boat may be pitching and tossing and it is difficult to handle the extinguisher with only one hand. Most regulations concerned with fire-fighting equipment specify the minimum capacity of a fire extinguisher to be 2 gallons. Such exting-uishers are cumbersome and difficult to use when the boat is pitching in heavy seas.

Another problem with extinguishers is that they are rarely made to resist the corrosive marine atmosphere. Those normally available are made for use in offices and factories, and corrode fairly rapidly in a marine environment. Corrosion is more a risk due to the fact that they have to be positioned close to exits so that the crew do not have to enter the com-partment to reach the extinguisher. The only solution to the corrosion problem is careful maintenance, which entails greasing the exposed metal parts. The silicone grease aerosol is useful for this purpose.

For the areas outside the engine compartment, fire extinguishers can usually put out a fire. If a fire occurs, it is likely someone will be close at hand and the extinguisher provides a ready means of tackling the blaze as soon as possible. The crew should always be encouraged to do this, as the time wasted in summoning help can be vital. If the fire gets beyond the extinguisher's capabilities then the fire hose is the next line of attack. Such hose will often be used for washing the deck, perhaps unofficially as far as the regulations are concerned, but speed is still vital and the first hose which will reach will be used. For most fires a straightforward jet is suitable, for oil fires a fine spray must be used and special nozzles are available so that the jet can be changed at will. There is unlimited water available for firefighting, but if water is being pumped into the boat it will have to be pumped out as well, but it is not advisable for the same pump to do both jobs because of the risk of clogging.

Of course, the engine may have stopped or been stopped because of the fire and this is where the hand pump built into the system is vital. It does not have the capabilities of the engine driven pump, but it is better than nothing. The hose used for firefighting should be capable of reaching all parts of the boat.

As for lifesaving equipment, there are statutory requirements laid down for firefighting equipment for many types of fishing boat. While a boat has to carry the specified equipment, the responsible skipper will carefully examine problems of fire on board his boat and determine the best way and the best equipment to deal with it. Safety equipment of this type is non-productive. It does not help the boat to operate more efficiently and it does not help to catch any more fish. For this reason only the bare minimum is often carried, and therefore governments and insurance companies have found it necessary to specify minimum requirements.

Apart from the lifesaving and firefighting fields there are other items of equipment which can be carried to meet particular safety requirements. A radar reflector can help the boat to show up better on other vessels' radar screens, which means less risk of collision in fog. The smaller the boat, the more important a radar reflector becomes and it should be considered essential equipment on boats under 40 feet in length.

Steel boats produce a good radar echo, but small boats with a low profile are lost among the reflections from waves. Wooden and GRP boats produce very poor radar echoes, and it is only the larger sizes that have sufficient metal in the fittings to produce a readable echo.

The radar reflector should be mounted at least 15 feet above the waterline to give the best results, and it should be of adequate size. The larger the reflector the stronger the echo which will be returned. A reflector around 18 inches (45 cm) on each side should be adequate. It should be permanently fastened to the mast or wheelhouse top. If it is hung from a halliard, this will soon chafe through and the reflector will come crashing down.

In a different category is the sea anchor which can be used to keep the boat head to wind if there is an engine failure. A sea anchor can make the working conditions on board more comfortable when repairing the engine, and in severe weather it can reduce the chance of the boat capsizing. It is not an essential piece of equipment because a substitute can always be rigged from the fishing gear on board. All that is required is something which will hold the water when it is towed. The sea anchor is streamed from the bow on a strong line and the pull on the line keeps the boat head to wind. A sea anchor is more essential for smaller boats which are more vulnerable to capsizing.

Similar to the sea anchor, but used for a different purpose, is the drogue. Towed astern, it keeps the boat stern to the waves when crossing a dangerous bar and prevents the boat from broaching. The drogue is used by a few fishing boats working from harbours with a dangerous entrance. To be really effective the boat must be designed for its use, a 'double-ender' being the best. Special strong fittings must be included to take the strain. The drogue itself is a very strong canvas cone which could also serve as a sea anchor.

Leaks and holes in the hull demand urgent treatment to prevent the boat from sinking. Special collision mats and similar gear can be carried on board for the purpose, but suitable equipment such as bunk mattresses and hatch covers can be used in such an emergency. All sorts of equipment to cope with all sorts of anticipated emergencies can be carried but these happen so rarely that the gear, when wanted, cannot be found. Most of the equipment required in an emergency can be improvised from what is on board and it is sensible to think about what could be used in particular situations. The safety equipment on board should always be kept in sound condition. The maintenance required is not very time consuming, and one day it might be needed quickly. The main solution to most emergencies at sea is to be prepared.

CHAPTER 8

Deck and Fish Hold

On a fishing boat, the working areas are probably the most important parts. Handling the fishing gear efficiently can save much time and can reduce the risk of accidents. Handling the catch is equally important if it is to be kept in good condition and sold for a good price. The profit margins in fishing are small and it is only by careful attention to details in the layout of the deck and fish hold that fishing can be really successful.

It is not the purpose of this book to go into the wide variety of fishing methods and the gear used. Many excellent books have been written on the subject already and anyway, most fishermen have a good idea of how they intend to fish. This chapter looks at some of the general points which must be taken into consideration when planning the layout of the deck and fish hold or when making changes.

The position of the main deck equipment such as winches, pot haulers, gallows and gantries are fairly permanent once fitted. They can be moved, but it is not just a matter of drilling new bolt holes. The strain to which these units are subjected is such that it has to be passed on to the main structure of the boat by means of doubling plates and similar reinforcing. It may not be sufficient to bolt a trawl winch down to the deck beams. The beams may have to be reinforced to take the strain by fixing ties between the beams down to the keel or frames.

The principle of fastening any equipment subject to strain is to spread the loading over as wide an area as possible. While important on steel and wooden boats, it is particularly important on GRP boats. Not only should the loading in general be spread, but high local loadings such as occur around holding down bolts should be spread by the use of large washers or doubling plates.

The position of items other than the fishing gear should be considered when planning the deck layout. On smaller boats the access hatch to the engine compartment is often placed on deck, and even on larger boats hatches for the removal of the engine should be provided.

Then there are the hatches for the fish hold and the store. The demands on deck space are considerable and only careful planning will accommodate all the requirements.

Probably the most important decision which has to be made in relation to the deck is the position of the wheelhouse. In earlier designs the wheelhouse was placed aft and the foredeck was the working area. The current trend is to place the wheelhouse forward even on the smallest fishing boats. The large clear aft deck makes the positioning of equipment easier. Working aft, the crew and equipment are better protected, but the wheelhouse forward is more exposed to the sea and must therefore be strongly built. The accommodation forward is more uncomfortable because of the increased motion, but fishing capability always takes priority over comfort.

The open fishing boat is fast disappearing and decked craft, even in boats 20 feet long, are now widely used. The deck is placed above the waterline and made watertight and self-draining. This adds greatly to the safety of the boat as water cannot easily find its way down below, but if it is to be effective all of the deck openings must be capable of being made watertight as well.

Hatches in the deck are necessary and the hatch to the fish hold has to be open at sea to receive the catch. Because the decks are often awash, the hatch is fitted with a raised coaming so that water cannot easily run down below. This hatch should be watertight, and to many designers this appears to mean the fitting of a heavy cover secured by a multitude of clamps. This is commendable and such a cover is capable of withstanding seas breaking over it, but simply because it is so heavy and difficult to manage, it is often left open at sea when it ought to be closed. In addition, the weight of the hatch can make it dangerous to handle at sea and the clamps which secure the hatch can foul ropes.

This bad design is seen frequently on fishing boats and its inclusion is often reinforced by safety regulations which insist on such heavy hatches. If a hatch is to be effective it must, of course, be watertight but it must also be simple and easy to open and close so that it will be kept closed when the conditions demand it. Therefore it is probably better to fit two smaller hatches instead of one large one, which could give the advantage of better stowage in the fish hold. This will be discussed in more detail later.

Engine hatches, if open to the deck, must be watertight. This demands extra care in their construction, as a little sea water running down into the engine compartment may cause rapid corrosion, and if it comes into contact with electrical equipment it will cause more serious trouble. As far as practicable the engine hatch should be

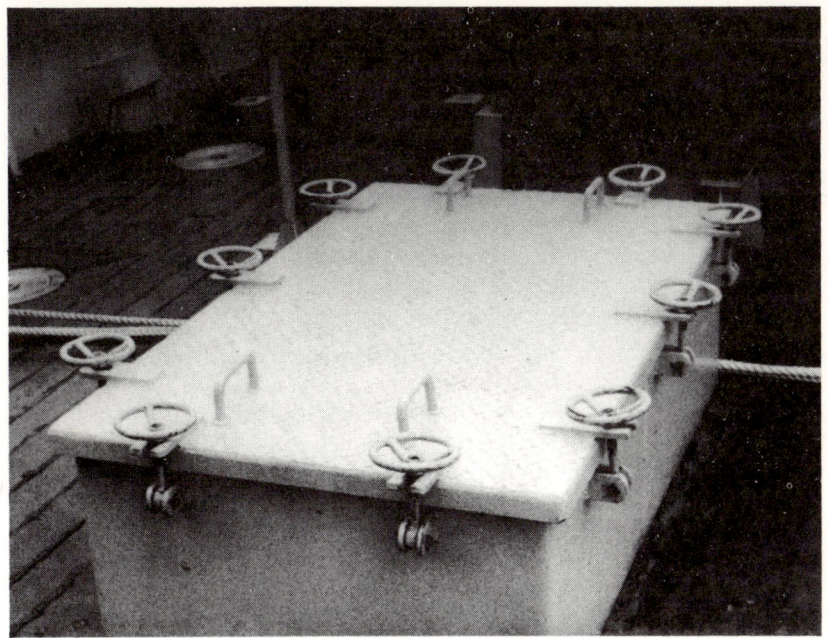

Fig 43   A fish hold hatch which will certainly keep the sea out but which will be very
difficult to handle at sea and ropes are likely to foul on the securing clamps.

positioned where the opening will be protected should the hatch be
opened at sea for repairs or maintenance.

The height of hatch coamings should be at least one foot (30 cm) to
stop water finding its way down easily when the hatch is open. However, a low hatch coaming is very easy to trip over, and a height of
two feet (60 cm) would be better from a safety point of view. At this
height, the coaming also provides something to brace against.

A self-draining deck requires some means of allowing the water to
drain off. Fishing boats are almost universally fitted with bulwarks
which offer added protection to the working area but with holes cut
in them for draining purposes. Not only do these holes or freeing
ports have to cope with the water which slops on deck and water
from washing down, but they have to be of such a size that they will
rapidly clear the water should a wave break over the bulwarks.

Many safety regulations specify the total area of the freeing ports to
ensure rapid clearance (see appendix), but these figures should be considered to be the minimum, because the ports have to be spread out
along the bulwark and they may not all be in use at one time. It is

common to concentrate the freeing ports at the lowest parts of the deck when the boat is static, although when the boat is pitching any water on deck may be concentrated at the forward or aft end of the deck. Freeing ports in the transom can be particularly effective for clearing water because the forward momentum of the boat tends to make the water drain aft.

However, freeing ports at the forward end of the deck must not be ignored. A wave coming over the stern or the quarter can be particularly devastating as the water will run forward, putting the bow down and making steering difficult. Large freeing ports at the forward end of the deck of a stern trawler will help to reduce the impact of this water, and on a boat with a whale back fitted over the forecastle such freeing ports are equally essential.

One problem with freeing ports is that as well as letting water out, they will also let it in, if they are just simple holes in the bulwark, which can make it uncomfortable for those working on deck. Closing doors are sometimes fitted to the ports, hinged near the top so that they are normally shut and cannot swing inboard. They form in effect, non–return valves allowing the water out but not in. If these are to work effectively they have to be maintained by oiling or greasing the hinges regularly.

Because freeing ports let water out they will also let out fish free on the deck, and for this reason they are often fitted with blanking plates to shut them off when the catch is on deck. This is permissible because the sea conditions are not likely to be extreme when fishing. However, these blanking plates are sometimes left in and are to be seen even rusted in position, forming a potentially dangerous situation. An alternative to blanking plates is to fit closely spaced bars across the freeing port hole which leaves it open for water to flow through but should help stop the fish. The effectiveness of this depends on the size of fish handled and, of course, the freeing port will have to be made larger to compensate for the area taken up by the bars.

Freeing ports are difficult to design to meet their conflicting requirements and the best efforts of a designer will be nullified if the fisherman stows gear by the hole so that it is effectively blocked. Pound boards on the deck to hold the catch while it is sorted can also prevent a clear flow of water, and this should also be considered when they are designed.

The height of the bulwarks is one of the factors used to determine the area of freeing ports required. In recent years the tendency has been to increase the height of bulwarks to give better protection to the crew working on deck, but this adds to the problem of clearing water from the decks. On the other hand, bulwarks should not be too low otherwise there is risk of a crewman being catapulted overboard if he loses his balance.

A low bulwark may be required for easy working of the gear, but this

Fig 44   High pound boards and boxes stowed on deck all increase the chance of water being held on deck to the detriment of the stability.

could be topped with a rail. There is much to commend a rail along the top of the bulwark whatever its height, as it provides a handhold, but in the immediate working areas it would be very prone to damage. There is no simple solution to the conflicting requirements of bulwarks, and each boat needs to be considered on its particular method of operation.

Water on deck means that openings in the superstructure must be watertight. Doors to the wheelhouse or accommodation should both be strong enough to withstand the onslaught of waves and at the same time, tight enough to prevent the water finding its way in. The same difficulty arises here as with deck hatches. A door which is both strong and water-tight is heavy and difficult to open and close.

A proper watertight door seals onto a rubber seal, and pressure is applied by four or more clamps around the edge of the door. These clamps usually operate independently but on more sophisticated doors there is a mechanism to allow them to be operated by a single lever or wheel. Passing through the door is often difficult, particularly if the boat is rolling heavily, when the door must be held in the open position in stepping over the wash step. Unless sea conditions are very bad the door is often hooked or tied open so that the whole purpose of the watertight door is lost.

Fig 45   Increasing use is being made of watertight doors on fishing boats to prevent water getting below. This type of door allows single handed operation.

The need for a completely watertight door is questionable. If the door opens onto the deck some dampness will be carried in on boots and oilskins anyway. The amount of water which will get past a close fitting wooden door is small and a simple knob and catch for normal use can be supplemented by a clamp for use when sea conditions are bad. Such a door must obviously be strong, but good design does not mean that a strong door must be heavy.

On a larger boat it is possible to vary the position of superstructure doors so that they can be placed in the most protected positions. They can open into areas where a small amount of water coming through the door will not do any harm. On smaller boats the doors usually open directly into the wheelhouse, and there is little choice as to where they are placed. The aft side of the wheelhouse is common, but the starboard side is sometimes chosen to give ready access to a pot hauler. With wheelhouse doors, care should be taken to keep electronic and electrical apparatus as far away as possible from the opening, and to arrange the door so that it gives protection to the opening when it is opened.

Doors from the accommodation or wheelhouse to the outside deck must be fitted with a wash board at the bottom. This prevents the water which is slopping about the deck from entering even when the door is open. Logically, this should be the same height as any hatches on deck, but this could also make the door difficult to negotiate. A height of around one foot (30 cm) is normally acceptable.

When planning the working layout of the aft deck, great care must be taken to get the leads for wires and ropes to winches and line haulers as fair as possible. Obviously, the fewer lead blocks in use the better, because each block adds to the total friction of the system and is something extra to maintain. Fixed lead blocks are preferable to the swinging type, but because they are fixed, the angle should be correct. The owner himself should be present at the yard when these leads are being worked out because it needs the practical experience of the man who is going to work them to position them correctly.

The working wires and lines should be kept as clear as possible from men who are working on deck and certainly men should not have to stand in the bight of a block. A failure of the wire or block could cause a nasty accident. Working gear such as blocks often do not receive the required maintenance on a fishing boat and failures occur. Indeed, it seems to be the philosophy of some fishermen to keep using gear until it breaks.

Blocks and rollers should always be fitted with nipples to ensure that they can be lubricated properly, but wear also takes place in unexpected places. Shackles and block eyes wear in the nips through the constant motion of the boat. Little can be done to reduce this except to tie the blocks up when they are not in use to prevent them swinging about. The wear is often hard to detect because it is well hidden and this emphasizes the need for regular and close inspection of the gear.

With the current trend towards reducing the number of the crew who are needed to work a fishing boat, the positioning of the controls for the deck machinery is important. One man can seldom be spared to work the controls only; he may also have to handle the engine controls and wheel, or, in the case of a line hauler, coil down the rope and handle the pots or hooks at the same time. Hydraulic drives with their simple control valves have made this duplication possible, and because the control valve can be placed remote from the machinery, the person in control can be situated in the best position.

For the trawl winch, the control valve is usually placed at the winch itself, but a secondary control or emergency stop can also be located in the wheelhouse. The control of line and pot haulers is usually local, and because the attitude of the boat needs to be adjusted when hauling, a console housing rudder, engine and hydraulic controls is often placed forward close by the hauler, when the wheelhouse is placed aft. On

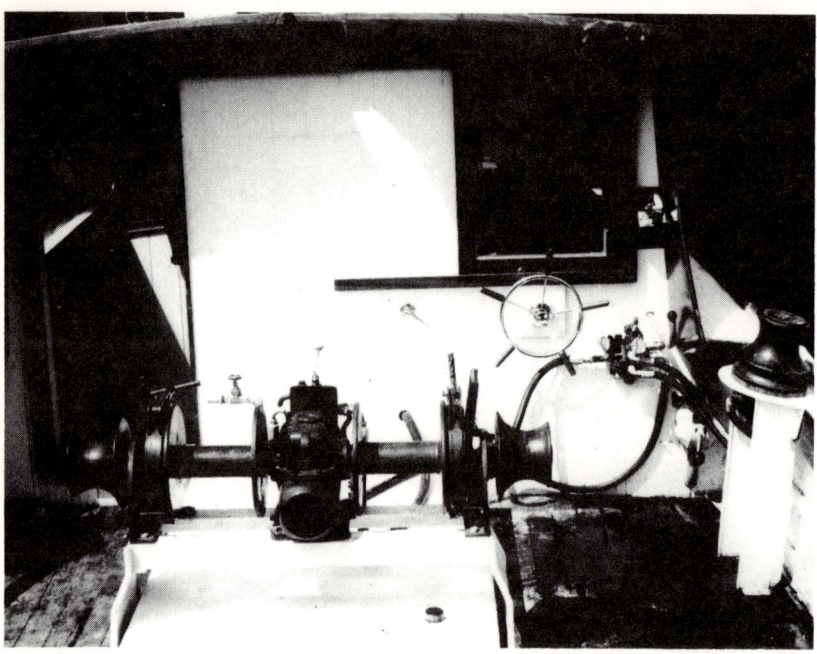

Fig 46   Deck machinery on a combination lobster boat/trawler. Both work from the same hydraulic pump which reduces the cost. The outside steering position and engine controls allow one man operation.

114

Fig 47   A net drum powered by a rope led to the main winch. The rope is wound around the
narrow side drum and when this is hauled the net drum turns. A simple and cheap
solution.

forward wheelhouse boats, the engine and rudder controls are close at
hand in the wheelhouse, which saves duplication, but this layout can limit
the working space around the hauler.

Accidents with trawl winches are frequent. Working with wires on a
moving deck makes such accidents almost inevitable at times, but they can
be reduced if there is someone at the winch controls all the time. An
additional safeguard is provided if these controls are duplicated, perhaps in
the wheelhouse, so that if an accident occurs to the winchman, there
should be someone close at hand to stop the winch. All trawl winches
should be reversible so that if there is an accident, there is some prospect of
sorting it out without too much difficulty.

One cause of accidents on fishing boats is the lack of handholds for the
crew. Often the boat will take a sudden, heavier than normal roll, and if
there is no hand hold nearby to seize, a man can be thrown across the deck.
It is worth considering fitting lifelines around the deck if they can be
accommodated without interfering with the working of the boat. The use
of a fixed rail above the bulwarks can be a great help as it serves the purpose
of having something to hold when moving about the deck.

The possibility of attaching a permanent rail around the winch or other hauling equipment should be considered. If carefully planned, this need not interfere with the free working of the winch, but it could offer useful protection for a crew member who loses his balance. In the same way a crew member who is working a rope around a drum, such as when hauling the cod end on board, needs something to brace himself against. If he loses his balance it could be unfortunate both for himself and for other crew members handling the net.

The need for suitable hand holds cannot be emphasized too strongly, not just on deck but in all parts of the boat. Equally important is good visibility about the deck so that each crew member can see what is going on. It should be possible to have a clear view of the deck from the wheelhouse whether this is placed forward or aft.

From this discussion it should be apparent that much thought and planning is required in designing a deck area which is easy and safe to work on. As fishing boats become more mechanized, more space on deck is required for machinery such as net drums and transducer line haulers, and the risk of accidents increases. When winches were belt driven from the main engine there was a trend to fit the winch into the lower part of the superstructure. There is no reason why this should not be done with a

Fig 48   The clear working deck of a lobster boat. Note the duplicate engine controls on the capstan pedestal.

116

hydraulic winch. It leaves more space on deck, but it involves incorporating a feeding device into the winch so that the trawl wire feeds onto the drum evenly.

The winch is better protected when placed in the superstructure, but the space it occupies may interfere with the provision of comfortable accommodation. Much will depend on whether the boat is at sea for extended periods or is engaged only on day fishing.

In planning the deck layout, take into account the amount of spare gear to be carried on board. Spare nets, fish boxes, baskets, ropes, fenders, all have to be stowed and despite the provision of below deck stores on board most boats, much of this gear remains stowed on deck because of the labour involved to stow it away after use each time. There is more likelihood of gear being stowed away if the stores are incorporated at deck level. This can be done where there is a raised forecastle, or perhaps a store under a raised wheelhouse. If the gear has to be carried on deck, proper provision should be made for it, rather than allow it to be stored around the winch or in other places where it can obstruct the working areas.

There are differences of opinion between fishing boat owners about lifting and hauling gear for the nets. The wide variety of arrangements to be seen on fishing boats is testimony to this, and the conclusion to be drawn is that the arrangements are rarely completely satisfactory. This is one of the major areas of experimentation on fishing boats and many boatyards have their own identifiable systems.

On trawlers, much of the experimentation has stemmed from the change from side to stern trawling. Initially, this involved simply moving the gallows aft to a position on each side of the transom. To brace these satisfactorily, they were joined across at the top, and this led to a 'goalpost' gantry arrangement. The modern trend appears to be to connect this goalpost to the mast by means of a fixed derrick. The mast is supported by means of fixed tubular supports, and the whole structure becomes rigid and self-supporting.

If such a structure is to work successfully it must be carefully stressed so that it is strong enough to meet the loads applied at the various lifting points, also as light as possible in the interests of maintaining good stability characteristics. Many fishermen adapt their fishing methods as they gain experience with a particular boat such as changing leads and hauling points, and in doing so they may overload the structure unless the changes are carefully planned.

The structure is usually built up from tubular members with the goalpost section often constructed from square section steel to give increased strength at the towing points. All the lifting and towing points should be fitted as low as possible, because when gear is being lifted, the weight being lifted is placed effectively at the lifting point on the derrick or goalpost. The effect of this on the stability characteristics of the boat must be considered. The towing point for the trawl also affects stability which can be particularly detrimental when the boat is turning.

Steel is normally used for the goalpost/derrick/mast structure, but in the interests of weight saving and stability aluminium has been used on several craft. Aluminium reduces maintenance because it does not corrode if it is the right grade, but the connections to the deck have to be carefully insulated from steel plating if electrolytic corrosion is to be avoided. There will always be a minor problem in this respect if steel blocks and fittings are used on the structure. The same applies to aluminium when used for deckhouses, but there are acceptable insulation methods for attaching these satisfactorily to a steel hull.

Where there is a fixed rigid structure there is no requirement for rigging to support the mast. Where rigging is used, it is worth investing in the stainless steel variety because corrosion can quickly ruin ordinary galvanized wire rigging unless it is well maintained. The tensioning screws for the rigging usually suffer the same fate, and here again stainless steel is a worthwhile investment.

However carefully the lifting and hauling systems are planned, at some time or other there will probably be a problem at sea. This will mean climbing up to sort things out and there should be a simple and safe way of getting to all the blocks and fittings on the structure, even when the boat is rolling about. Steel rungs are normally fitted, which are quite adequate for most purposes, provided that they are carefully positioned. So often one finds that the next rung up is difficult to reach or there is not room to stand on both feet when trying to unravel things. The provision of easy access to the mast and fittings also means that these are likely to receive better maintenance when in harbour.

The same degree of care and thought which is required in planning the deck layout and working areas should also be given to planning the fish hold. Much will depend on the layout of the boat, the species of fish being handled and the duration of the trips, but as with most small fishing boats, the emphasis must be on versatility so that changes from one type of fishing to another can be made readily.

The position of the fish hold depends on the position of the engine compartment and vice versa. Which takes priority depends a great deal on the individual designer and owner, but because the weight carried in the fish hold will vary as the trip progresses, it is logical to position the fish hold as near to the centre of gravity of the boat as possible, so that the variations in the weight carried in the fish hold will have little effect on the trim of the boat. If the fish hold is placed well aft, ballast tanks which can be adjusted to maintain a suitable trim have to be provided. This is an unnecessary complication and generally indicates bad design.

The problem is whether to place the engine compartment forward or aft of the fish hold. The general trend is to place the engine under the wheelhouse. This has the advantage of short engine controls and access to the engine can be gained from inside the wheelhouse. In either case, the fish hold tends to be placed towards one end of the boat or the other, but with modern diesel engines and gearboxes becoming more compact it is becoming easier to fit the machinery close up to the stern tube. This can simplify the arrangements greatly, whether the boat is a stern trawler or has the wheelhouse aft.

Having the engine aft keeps all the machinery together because the steering gear is in the same compartment, but more important from the construction point of view, it only means one fireproof and water-proof bulkhead between the engine and the rest of the boat. In addi-tion, the propeller shaft does not have to run under the fish hold, sim-plifying maintenance and providing more room in the hold.

The requirements of the fish hold are many and conflicting. There must be access to the deck to allow fish to be put below for storage at sea and for discharging the catch in harbour. The space within the hold should be divided, except on small boats, so that the fish boxes can be secured to prevent movement at sea, yet at the same time it must be simple to stow the boxes. Hygiene must be maintained to ensure that the catch is kept in good condition and that there is no chance of contamination by oil, grease or fuel. Lastly, the damp atmosphere is very corrosive to metal and conducive to producing rot in timber.

Whether or not the fish hold is insulated, it should at least be lined, not just to keep the boxes away from the side of the boat, but to make a good seal so that the water and fish slurry can be drained into a well for pumping out. Tongued and grooved timber is the tradi-tional method, and provided it is well fitted it can make an adequate seal. Problems arise when the timber starts to rot in the damp atmos-phere. Old fishing boats rarely have fish hold linings in good condi-tion. Marine quality plywood is also used for lining, and this is more durable, but the absorbent surface of the wood is difficult to keep clean and requires frequent painting.

Metal sheeting is also used to line fish holds, but careful fitting is required if it is to be satisfactory. The metals are galvanized iron sheet-ing or aluminium, with the latter being preferred. Galvanized iron itself has good corrosion resistance, but where the edges have to be cut to make the sheets fit and where holes have to be drilled, corrosion starts. For fastening sheets of all types, stainless steel screws are the only really satisfactory method although galvanized nails are perhaps an alternative and are much simpler and cheaper. Do not use the latter for aluminium sheeting.

A modern system is to line the hold with GRP either in the form of fitted sheets, or more commonly as a coating on a timber lining. In this way, the fish hold can be completely sealed with a durable coating which can be easily repaired should it be damaged. Accidental damage is the main problem with most fish hold linings. They are satisfactory when fitted, but once they are damaged or start to rot and little attempt made to rectify the situation, it will become worse in a very short time. A small section of damaged GRP will allow water to enter the timber underneath and soon the bond between the wood and the GRP breaks down.

The partitions within fish holds are usually portable or semi-portable, with boards being fitted into slots to separate areas. The boards may be of timber, plastic (including GRP) or aluminium. Timber boards are prone to swelling when wet and are liable to stick

Fig 49   The fish hold of a steel fishing boat, insulated then lined with GRP to give a clean hygienic surface.

in their grooves. Plastic and aluminium are both satisfactory provided they are well made, with the aluminium pattern being of the extruded type rather than the pressed sheet type. Quality is costly, but so often the fish hold is looked on as an area where economies can be made because it is not exposed to the sea. This is false economy.

Much of the damage caused to both the linings and the boards and their fittings stems from moving heavy boxes of fish around in the hold, particularly at sea where a box may slide about due to the rolling of the boat. Much of this could be avoided, and the whole process of fish stowage made much easier, if fixed (or at least semi-permanent) boxes were used.

The boxes could be filled by means of a movable chute extending from the deck. This could be designed so that it can extend to all parts of the hold, thus enabling the boxes to be filled in situ. With the boxes firmly located in position there is no risk of them moving about when the boat rolls, possibly affecting the stability of the boat. For discharging in harbour the boxes could be simply unfastened and swung ashore.

With such a system the fish would be in better condition because they would be handled less, simply picked from the deck and dropped down the chute. There would be no need to open up the hatches, admitting warmer air, and risking water getting down below if a wave came on board when the hatches were off.

Except on small boats it is unlikely that one chute would be sufficient to reach all parts of the fish hold, and it may be advantageous to divide up fish holds anyway. With a longitudinal bulkhead there is less risk if the fish boards give way. At least all the catch will not be hurled to one side on a heavy roll, and dividing the hold means providing two hatches which could speed up the process of unloading. With the hatches placed on each side of the deck rather than on the centre line, the important working area is kept clear.

The suggestion of a chute for stowing fish in the fish hold is just one possibility which may solve some of the problems of stowage. It is evident that there is room for improvement for the stowage of fish in the fish hold and this seems to have been a very neglected area of fishing boat design. Built-in permanent stowages which have to be filled in a fixed sequence offer the possibility of controlled loading of the catch. By ensuring the correct distribution of the cargo in the boat, the possibility of a dangerous loss of stability through alteration of the centre of gravity could be avoided. The stability situations could be pre-calculated.

There are various methods of insulating the fish hold. The insulating material should not be prone to rot or fungus growth and it must be non-absorbent, because however well the lining is secured leaks will occur in time. The materials generally used for insulation are cork, loose fibreglass mat, and polyurethane foam. This latter material can either be foamed in situ or cut into blocks and fitted. Cork can be either granular or cut into blocks.

Cork is fast becoming obsolete because of its high cost. The blocks are preferable to the granular form, which can leak out if a hole is knocked in the lining. Polyurethane foam should expand to fill all the cavities within the insulation space, but voids often occur due to trapped air. Foam lining in the hull like this can also make repairs to the hull difficult as it must be cut out to obtain access.

If the hull flexes, foam in situ can break up. The same foam inserted in block form is more durable, but it will rub away if there is any movement in the hull. It is more suitable for steel and GRP hulls than wood. One disadvantage of foam is that in a fire it produces toxic fumes which could greatly add to the difficulties.

In general, fibreglass mat is probably the best material to use. It is similar to that used for insulating homes and it can be used to insulate cabins and the superstructure to help maintain an even temperature. One advantage of this material is that it allows a small degree of air circulation which is necessary on a wooden boat to help reduce the chance of rot attacking the boat's timbers behind the lining. If no insulation is fitted to the fish hold it is worth taking care to ensure a good flow of air between the planking and the lining. The greatest proportion of rot and corrosion which attack fishing boats occurs in these areas.

In the design of the fish hold care should be taken to ensure that water can drain freely from all parts of the hold to the bilge suction point. A concrete filling is often placed in the bottom of the fish hold, but if this is to work efficiently it must make a good seal where it meets the side of the boat. The concrete should be put in when the boat is lying afloat so the correct drainage slopes can be gauged.

Some fishing boats engaged in catching shellfish are experimenting with storage tanks built into the hull to keep their catch alive, particularly if fishing keeps them at sea for more than a day. These storage tanks are of two types: those where sea water is allowed to flow in and out at will as the boat moves through the water and those working on a closed system where the water is artificially oxygenated.

The first type is a tank, usually integral with the hull. It is often built in the shape of a cone with the pointed end upwards terminating in a hatch through which the lobsters are put in and removed. This shape is chosen because it minimizes the area of the free liquid surface which, if large, could have a detrimental effect on the boat's stability.

The level of the water in the tank will be the same as that of the outside water, because the tank is connected to the outside by means of holes in the hull which are mesh covered to prevent the shellfish escaping. Of course, the hatch must be placed well above the water line.

The second type of tank can be either integral or separate, but the same sort of shape is used or baffles are fitted to prevent surge. In this type of tank a small air compressor is used to pump air into the tank to replenish the oxygen. The advantage of this type of tank is that it is self-contained so that the fish cannot be contaminated by the boat passing through polluted water. The water in the system can also be cooled if required, which can reduce the mortality of certain species in warm weather. With the closed system, no parts of the system should be made from metal with a copper content so brass and bronze fittings cannot be used. The tank itself is normally constructed from GRP to prevent corrosion problems.

Most fisheries have developed their own fishing and storage techniques by experience. This does not mean that they cannot be improved upon, and one of the reasons for a very slow process of change in the fishing world is the insular attitude of many fishermen. To look and study what other fishermen are doing or just to try and make an objective assessment of one's own fishing methods can often show new avenues worth exploring. Most of the new techniques in fishing, including the stern trawler itself, came about because people were not satisfied with their existing fishing methods. They went back to first principles and thought it out from the beginning. There must be many improvements still to come, and starting on a new boat is a good time to look for these improvements.

CHAPTER 9

Wheelhouse and Accommodation

The wheelhouse and accommodation are discussed together because on the smaller boats they tend to merge into one, and even on the larger boats covered by this book, the galley and messroom are often to be found at the aft end of the wheelhouse. This arrangement saves space.

Some disadvantages of this arrangement are found at night when lights are needed in the galley section. These will be reflected from the wheelhouse windows and make it difficult to keep a good lookout. A close fitting curtain can probably stop most of the galley light but if good night visibility is to be obtained, something must be done to obscure the various pilot and indicator lights which are fitted to radios and other electronic equipment. There should be some way of switching these off or blanking them over so that they do not intrude at night.

If lights are required in the wheelhouse at night they should be red. This colour does not affect night vision nearly as much as white lights, and is commonly used for chart table lighting. One advantage of the forward sloping windows found on many fishing boats is that they minimize reflections as they will only reflect light from the deck head. If the deck head is painted black it should be possible to see out quite clearly.

The forward sloping windows were first introduced to give a clear view of what was happening on the fore deck. They are not so necessary from this point of view on a stern trawler, but there should be similar windows at the aft end of the wheelhouse so that the skipper has a clear view of the aft deck. Some boats have fitted another set of engine and steering controls at this point with the winch controls.

Visibility is equally important from the wheelhouse windows in fog, frost, rain and snow or when there is a lot of spray. This problem can be solved simply by having windows which open, but in the interests of comfort and of keeping the electrical and electronic equipment in the wheelhouse dry, it is now common practice to

124

Fig 50   The simple wheelhouse on a small inshore boat. The enclosed radar scanner prevents it being fouled by ropes.

fit windscreen wipers or clear view screens to one or more of the windows.

Each of these clearing systems has its merits. The clear view screen keeps its area of glass extremely clear under most conditions, but the clear area is limited in size and has the disc hub obstructing the centre. The wiper, provided it is one designed for marine use, will clear a larger area but will smear the glass if there is only a little spray to clear. This can be corrected by fitting fresh water screen washers, and wipers seem to be more popular than the clear view screen. Both types tend to have noisy electric motors, and it would be a better idea if manufacturers could make these quieter. The wiper blade swinging to and fro can induce sleepiness during a long watch.

For working in cold regions some form of demister may be necessary to keep the windows clear. This could be hot air ducted from a radiator in the engine cooling system or from the boat's heating system. Electrical heaters are available which can be built into a clear view screen. In favour of the hot air system is the fact that it also serves to heat the wheelhouse itself, but it tends to act as a demister rather than to clear ice off the window. A demister is very necessary if the galley is situated in the wheelhouse.

The wheelhouse is the centre of operations of the fishing boat and much information is provided to the skipper to help him make the right decisions. This information comes in many forms and unless the layout of the wheelhouse is carefully planned there is likely to be confusion. On larger boats there is now so much equipment that it is worth making a model of the interior of the wheelhouse so that it can all be arranged before construction starts.

The layout depends on assessment of priorities. Two main functions are carried out in the wheelhouse: finding fish and that of general navigation. The former is carried out on the fishing grounds, normally away from hazards in the form of rocks and shoals, while the latter function is operated on the way to and from the grounds and on entering harbour. Current practice is to place the emphasis on the fish finding aspect, leaving the general navigation to be carried out as well as possible in the circumstances. This overlooks the fact that the fish caught is only worth money when it has been landed and quick safe passages to and from the fishing grounds are just as important as catching fish. An attempt therefore should be made to separate the two functions as far as possible, but much will depend on the size of the wheelhouse. It is better to have the general navigation area at the forward end of the wheelhouse and the fish finding area towards the rear, with the instruments which are required for both (such as Decca Navigator or Loran) somewhere in between. Alternatively, they could be side by side if the wheelhouse is wide enough.

The operation of fish finding equipment is much the same irrespective of weather conditions, but with general navigation, the pressure on the helmsman or skipper can be greatly increased as the weather deteriorates. During poor visibility, radar is one of the most important instruments and this must be placed where it can be used effectively for long periods at a time. If it is to be used efficiently, it must be comfortable to operate. Other navigation equipment is less critical and the information presented can be taken in with less concentration. The use of the Decca Navigator or echo sounders is intermittent, but also requires a space where a chart can be laid out.

The operation of fish finding equipment needs as much concentration as the radar when fishing is being carried out. Sometimes fishing has to be carried out in fog, which can put heavy demands on a one-man operation and this is where a carefully planned layout can provide most benefits.

Non-essentials should be taken out of the main operation area. For example, engine gauges are not essential if alarms are fitted. All the

Fig 51 The wheelhouse of a steel fishing boat. The Decca Navigator on the right has a good chart space aft of it. The mirror above the centre window reflects the compass readings from a compass on the wheelhouse top where there is less magnetic influence.

less important instruments such as fuel tank content gauges can be positioned out of the wheelhouse, or at least installed where they will not cause confusion. The simpler the wheelhouse, the less chance there will be of making a mistake.

When deciding on the arrangement of the model, allow for the fact that the wheelhouse will not always be steady and level. At sea, it will be rolling and pitching, and so strong hand holds must be provided. Try moving about in the model to find the natural position of hand holds. They should also be placed around equipment such as the radar or fish finders. This equipment can only be operated well if it is comfortable to use.

Hand holds must be strong and fastened by bolts and not screws. It is surprising just how much strain a hand hold has to take. Some

Fig 52   Clutter in a fishing boat's wheelhouse. This sort of unplanned layout can be very inefficient and lead to mistakes. Only the important items should be fitted close to the wheel.

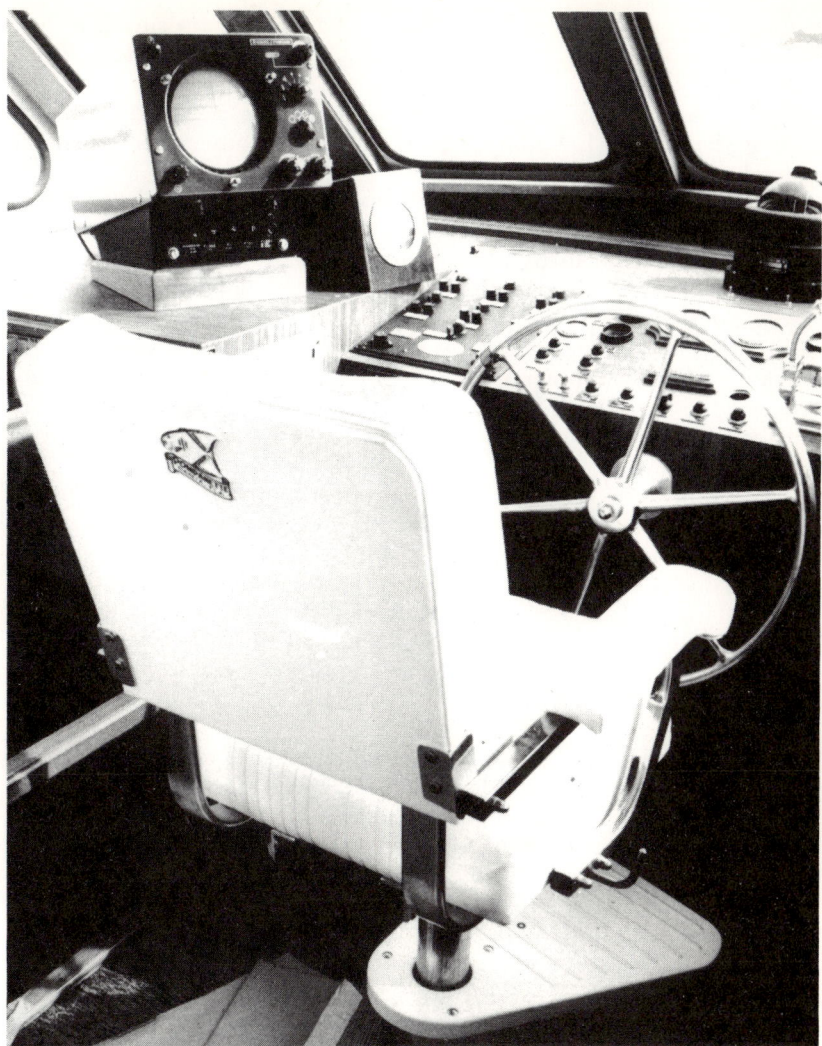

Fig 53 A comfortable chair at the steering position but it would have been better if the wheel had been angled, otherwise the helmsman's knees get in the way.

equipment is provided with built-in hand holds, but these may not be strong enough to take this strain.

A chair for the skipper is now becoming a common fitment on fishing boats, and has much to commend it. It must be strong and well secured, because it will take a great deal more strain than a similar seat ashore. It should be fitted with arms so that the person sitting in it is well supported against the movement of the boat. The problem with a seat is that it limits the amount of equipment which can be seen and operated comfortably by the seated person. It is therefore probably best used in the fish finding area in the wheelhouse rather than the general navigation area.

On small fishing boats the wheelhouse often appears to be added as an afterthought and only as offering protection for the helmsman. This may be true of many older boats, but with the increasing sophistication of even small boats the helmsman is surrounded with all sorts of complicated equipment. To meet this demand the equipment tends to be fitted into all available spaces with little thought for the efficient operation of the equipment. There is no reason to suppose that fishing boats of the future will be any less complex and it is likely that there will be even more equipment installed in the ever increasing need to locate fish.

The lesson to be learnt from this in planning the wheelhouse layout is that there should always be space left for the installation of more equipment.

The same approach is needed for planning the accommodation. Whereas a few years ago a couple of bunks and a bucket might have been adequate, now crews are demanding all the comforts of home. The time cannot be far away when legislation will require certain minimum standards of crew accommodation, even on small boats, so it is as well to think ahead in this respect when building a new boat.

The accommodation is usually located at one end of the boat or the other, largely because this space is not much use for anything else. It is inevitable that the machinery and the fish hold will take priority as regards space within the hull, because these areas help to earn money. Legislation may force a change in these priorities, but wherever the accommodation is placed within the hull, much can be done to make it comfortable and practical. Yacht designers, who are experts in fitting more and more accommodation into less and less space can provide good examples.

Most of the time spent in the accommodation will be spent sleeping so the bunks should have priority. As much privacy as possible should be given to the individual sleeping quarters, not so much in the interests of modesty, although with women taking to the sea this may be necessary, but to cut down the disturbance to those sleeping. If space permits the accommodation to be divided up into small cabins, this should be done because there is less disturbance when one person gets up.

The old style of box bunk is now giving way to more normal

bunks, but a good lee board is still required to help the person in the bunk to stay there when the boat is rolling about. Mattresses are now almost invariably made from foam and sleeping bags are used in place of blankets, as they are warmer and easier to handle.

It is very difficult to control the temperature effectively in a small cabin: it is either too hot or too cold. It should be possible to regulate the temperature fairly precisely and some form of thermostatic control is desirable. Ventilation is equally important to prevent the atmosphere from becoming stuffy and the two requirements could be combined in a warm air heater. In hot weather the fan can still be used to circulate air, and if the boat operates for long periods in warm climates then an air-conditioning unit could be a worthwhile investment. There are several types made for use on yachts, and these self-contained units are easy to install and cheap to run.

In fitting out accommodation, it should be made so that it is easy to keep clean and requires the minimum of maintenance. In selecting materials for the fitting out it should be borne in mind that some countries have legislation which demands the use of fireproof or fire-resistant materials for the accommodation, and this can severely restrict the choice of what can be used.

Here we must look at the special panelling materials developed for fitting out big ships where fire regulations are strictly enforced. This panelling material is usually based around an asbestos core and surfaced with a plastic material. It is expensive, but once fitted it is there for the life of the vessel, and for cleaning it only requires a wipe down.

The fitting has to be done carefully to avoid joints and cracks which could harbour dirt, and special framing systems are often available to make a simple and neat job. It is no good using this expensive material unless the supporting framework is built to the same standard. In panelling the side of the boat try to fit in some removeable panels so that the carrying out of a full survey of the hull does not involve ripping out the panelling. The same applies if wiring or piping is fitted behind the panelling.

The same panelling material can be used on the deckhead, but for the decks in the accommodation, alternative materials have to be used. On wood and GRP boats, these materials can be used in their bare state with perhaps a carpet covering, but with steel boats it is usual to apply some form of composition to the deck to act as both insulation and to form a non-slip surface. Here again, possible fire regulations may affect the choice of materials.

Some regulations demand that all fabrics such as curtains and carpets used in the accommodation are fire-proofed. This is prudent, as the majority of fires occurring in fishing boats start in the accommodation. A further point to bear in mind when designing the accommodation, is that two exits must be provided to each compartment. Apart from the main entrance, it is usual to fit an escape hatch in the deck head leading out onto the deck. There are some excellent designs of these hatches, developed for yachts, and in addition to providing a means of escape they can be used to provide additional light and ventilation down below.

Sound-proofing of the accommodation is necessary if the crew are to get a good rest. Good heat insulation fitted behind the panelling will do much to deaden the sound but special sound absorbing material may be necessary if the cabin is under the wheelhouse or working deck. The noise of the engine is best minimized by sound-proofing in the engine compartment itself. This is essential if the engine room is adjacent to the accommodation or is under the wheelhouse. The continual noise from an engine can be very wearying and, over a long period, can affect judgment.

The standard of the accommodation and the extent to which it is fitted out will largely depend on the type of fishing being carried out. For boats engaged on day fishing there is little need for much in the way of accommodation, but it is useful to have a bunk or two fitted in case it proves necessary to spend a night at sea because of a missed tide or through any other mishap. The pattern of fishing may change and require longer periods at sea. Therefore the boat should be adaptable.

Supplying adequate food on a fishing boat can be a major problem. Not only the preparation and the cooking of the food, but also the buying of supplies during the time the boat is in harbour can be very time consuming. Even on a boat which is day fishing, food is important, because a crew are likely to work better with good food. Sandwiches and thermos flasks can be used, but they become monotonous and there is much to be said in favour of 'proper' meals. Most boats have cooking facilities available, but only if these are supplemented by a refrigerator and possibly a deep freeze can full advantage be taken of the many pre-prepared foods available.

The defrosting time required for frozen foods can be overcome by using a microwave oven. This may sound an expensive solution to the problem, but consider the advantages. Frozen food can be taken direct from a deep freeze and cooked in a matter of minutes. The microwave oven also reduces the time required for cooking or heating conventional foods, leading to savings in fuel for cooking and in manpower, the latter being the main advantage. The fact that the food being cooked is shut up in the oven means there are no pots boiling on a

Fig 54 The galley is an important part of a fishing boat and it should be possible to prepare and cook good meals even with the boat moving about.

stove, always a source of accidents on a small boat in heavy seas.

Refrigerators on boats can work from either gas or electricity, the former having the advantage that it can continue to work in harbour. Deep freeze units are usually run by electricity, which might make them impractical unless the boat can connect to a shore electrical connection when in harbour. It is worth trying to arrange for this because a deep freeze can greatly simplify the problems of food stores for the boat.

The best accommodation is soon ruined if the crew come straight in from the deck in their working gear. If it can be arranged, it is a good idea to have a changing area immediately inside the door from the deck where oilskins and seaboots can be stowed. Such an area will help keep the accommodation clean and comfortable.

The carpeted decks in accommodation and wheelhouse found in many modern fishing boats are testimony to changing attitudes amongst fishermen. Not only are they looking for higher standards, but are prepared to do something about maintaining them. Future requirements must also be carefully borne in mind.

CHAPTER 10

Anchors, Ropes, Wires and Chains

Without ropes of one sort or another a fishing boat could not earn profits. Not only the ropes and wires used on the fishing gear itself, but all the various ropes needed for a ship to operate and the items of equipment used with the ropes such as anchors and blocks must be considered. With the variety of different materials from which ropes are made, a fisherman needs a good understanding of ropes and gear if he is to have the right rope for a particular job.

Every boat needs an anchor, and as it may be required in emergencies it should be kept ready for immediate use. Larger fishing boats may have the anchor stowed in a hawse pipe, or the bow roller may be adapted so that the anchor can be stowed there. The alternative is for the anchor to be stowed on deck. Wherever it is stowed it should be secure, because it is a heavy awkward object and could cause much damage if it breaks loose.

There is a variety of anchor designs to choose from. The stockless anchor and variations of this pattern will fit snugly into a hawse pipe and generally have good holding power in relation to their weight (particularly the Danforth). They are not so effective if the sea bed is rocky, but for a softer bottom they are very good. The CQR or plough anchor has similar qualities, but is less easy to stow on board.

An anchor which will hold on virtually all types of bottom, and thus one which is well suited for emergency use, is the fisherman's or Admiralty pattern anchor. This is the traditional type of anchor with a stock at right angles to the line of the flukes, which can be collapsed for ease of stowage.

A well equipped fishing boat would carry two anchors, perhaps a Danforth and a fisherman's. One of these, usually the Danforth, would be kept stowed on deck, with the anchor line attached, with the other stowed away but readily available for use. Anchors are heavily galvanized to reduce corrosion, but because they all contain some moving parts, some attention is required occasionally to prevent the hinges from seizing up, particularly if the anchor is rarely used.

Fig 55   An anchor peculiar to US boats which works well and stows easily, ready for immediate use.

Anchor lines can be of wire and chain, rope and chain or all chain. If a wire is used, this is usually the trawl wire. If the trawl wire is used in this way some provision must be made for suitable leads from the trawl winch to the forepart of the boat (easy to arrange on a side trawler, but not so simple on a stern trawler). The short length of chain, usually around 2 fathoms long, is used as additional weight to help the anchor to hold and to keep the pull on the anchor as near horizontal to the sea bed as possible, which helps the anchor to hold more securely.

A similar chain is used when rope is used for the anchor line. Even when the trawl wire is normally used for anchoring, a rope should be kept for use with the second anchor. Rope or wire is usually reserved for the smaller types of fishing boat, all chain anchor cables being used on larger craft. This chain should be of the short link type or stud link chain, both of which are free from kinking and snagging when it is stowed in a locker. When chain is used for the anchor a small windlass is usually fitted onto the foredeck to raise or lower it. This windlass may be hand operated, but it can also be powered by an hydraulic or electric motor. The anchor is normally let go on the brake, hauled in by power and stowed automatically below decks in the chain locker.

A chain will stand up to the wear and tear of lying on the sea bed better

135

Fig 56   A Danforth anchor with its chain and line. This equipment would meet the needs of many small fishing boats.

than a rope or wire if the boat has to anchor for any length of time. It will not chafe where it passes over the bow, whereas a rope could quickly wear through if the boat moves about, unless special precautions are taken against chafing. The shackles used to connect the anchor to the chain should be 'moused' if they are screw shackles, or otherwise dealt with so that there is no risk of them coming undone when the anchor is on the bottom.

136

Anchors and lines are often a much neglected part of the equipment on fishing boats, largely because they are rarely used. It pays to give them a little attention occasionally, because the time when the anchor might be needed could be when the engine has broken down and the boat is drifting onto a lee shore. The anchor can avert disaster long enough to enable the rescue boats to arrive.

The weight of the anchor will vary with the size of the boat. For a boat up to 30 feet long (10 m) an anchor weighing between 30 and 50 lb (14 and 23 kg) would be suitable. Above this size the weight of the anchor should increase so that a 60 foot (20m) boat needs an anchor of between 80 and 100 lb (36 to 45 kg). It becomes obvious why a motor is required to haul it up. One final point on anchors: always make the inboard end of the line or chain fast before letting go so that there is no chance of losing it all overboard.

Natural fibre ropes have in general been superseded by ropes made from synthetic materials. The natural fibres required a great deal more care because they were prone to rot if stored away damp, and they were larger in diameter, strength for strength, than the synthetic ropes. For a while natural fibre was cheaper but now that final advantage has gone. Some of the synthetic ropes available are now described.

Nylon — This was one of the first of the synthetic fibres to be made up into rope. Nylon is about three times as strong as manilla rope of the same diameter. It is very flexible, easy to handle rope but its smooth surface can make it difficult to grip. It is slightly less strong when wet, but is otherwise unaffected by water. Being heavier than water it will not float. It is a very elastic rope having good stretch and recovery characteristics, and is therefore excellent for mooring and anchor lines. It is damaged by heat and the surface fibres will melt if the rope is allowed to surge round bollards or a winch barrel when there is a heavy load on the rope.

Terylene (Dacron) – This rope has very similar properties to nylon in many respects except that it has low stretch properties, making it more suited to hauling lines such as tackles. Its strength is slightly less than that of nylon. Terylene is less flexible than nylon, but it is often made up in a braided form which has good flexibility and is easier to handle.

Polypropylene – One form of this rope is made up from short fibres rather in the manner of natural fibres and it combines many of the features of the natural ropes with the good rot resistance of the synthetic ropes. This rope is one of the few synthetic ropes which will float and it has a strength somewhere between that of manilla and nylon. Polypropylene is a good rope to handle and is used for many general purposes where high strength is not a critical feature.

Polyethylene – This rope is sold under many different names, such as

Courlene. It is a coarse floating rope with reasonable strength properties, but its main features are its resistance to abrasion and water. It is used much for fishing gear and moorings, but it is not an easy rope to handle, being stiff and slippery.

Kevlar — This material was originally developed for use as a base fabric for motor car tyres. Its use in rope is still in its infancy, but it shows such excellent strength properties that it could well be replacing steel wire for trawl lines in future years. The use of Kevlar in ropes is restricted to polyurethane coated types at present, with greatly improved resistance to abrasion. Trials are being carried out with a Kevlar rope with a braided nylon sheath which looks promising for use where high strength is required. At present, the high price of Kevlar is likely to restrict its use, but this price will probably fall as it comes into wider use.

All these synthetic ropes lose a degree of their strength when exposed to direct sunlight for long periods. This is only a problem in hotter climates and the loss is unlikely to reach significant proportions. It is wear and tear which will largely dictate the useful life of the rope. Rope is expensive and attention to a few basic points can do much to prolong its life.

Heat can damage ropes, so they should be kept away from hot areas such as near the galley stove outlet and the funnel or exhaust. It is surprising how often the engine exhaust on a fishing boat ejects close to ropes on the mast and this must reduce the life of the rope. This is something which can be avoided in the basic design of the boat.

Chafe and wear probably account most for shortening the life of a rope, and this is where careful planning of the deck layout can help. If a rope is led across another rope or a part of the boat's structure then it will wear rapidly. All changes in direction in a rope must be done round a lead block and even then there are certain requirements in the block to reduce the possibility of wear.

Many blocks used on fishing boats are too small for the rope they have to handle. One can only assume that these are fitted for reasons of economy but it is false economy because a small block will cause the rope to wear more quickly. There is a minimum curvature to which a rope should be subjected, and this is about six times the diameter of the rope. It is better to think in terms of ten times the diameter if possible, with the factor of six times being regarded as the absolute minimum. The block must also allow the rope to pass through freely so that it does not wear against the side plates, and the block must be free to take up the natural line of the rope to allow a fair lead.

With the hauling gear used on a fishing boat being normally rigged in fixed positions there should be no problem in allowing the ropes to run freely. Mooring ropes are a different problem, and very little thought seems to be given to prolonging the life of these expensive ropes. If there is any swell or surge running at the fishing boat's berth, then a rope can be ruined overnight.

The mooring arrangements on many fishing boats appear to be added as an afterthought with little attempt to ensure a good lead for the ropes. The stout wooden posts used on smaller boats and the steel 'bitts' used on larger boats are usually well secured, but it is where the rope leads over the side that troubles occur. Fair leads often belie their name and change the direction of the rope at far too sharp an angle for comfort. A similar rule applies here as for blocks, but a minimum radius of at least three times the diameter of the rope should be allowed.

Not only will a sharper bend weaken the rope, but any movement between the boat and the quay will set up a rubbing motion which will start to wear away the rope. If the boat always uses the same berth, it would be well to fit a plastic tube or some old canvas around the rope where the chafing occurs. This is one solution to the problem, but a better approach is to arrange the leads for the ropes between the boat and quay in such a way that they cannot rub.

Fair leads are a mixed blessing and often do more harm than good. As good strong bulwarks are fitted to most fishing boats, there is no reason why mooring posts cannot be fitted directly onto the bulwarks, thus allowing the lead to be taken straight ashore. On many trawlers, the gallows are used as a mooring point, but often these have sharp edges which can cut into the rope.

When considering mooring arrangements remember the possibility that the boat may have to be towed, or tow another vessel.

Forward, the bow roller, which is often fitted for mooring or anchoring purposes, can give a good lead. The roller itself must be of adequate diameter and the cheek plates on either side must be high enough to stop the rope jumping out of the lead. These rollers can be subjected to considerable strain so they should be strongly built. Having the lead directly from the roller to a stout post on the centre of the foredeck provides an arrangement which will be quite adequate for most towing, anchoring or mooring requirements.

Aft, the arrangements are complicated by the fishing requirements or by the wheelhouse. For towing, the securing point for the tow line should be some way in from the transom, but it is rarely possible to achieve this, and mooring and towing facilities are usually restricted to a strong post in each corner of the transom. For most purposes, this is satisfactory.

While a natural fibre or synthetic rope will only be weakened temporarily if it passes through a sharp bend and it will recover completely, this is not so with a wire rope. A sharp bend can cause a kink which will permanently weaken the rope, so wire must be treated with even greater respect than ropes. A wire bent to a curve, which is not much bigger than the diameter of the wire, will lose over 50% of its strength.

For a wire to have long life, large diameter blocks must be used and if the speed of hauling is fast, say more than 200 feet per minute (60 m), which can be achieved by some trawl winches, then even larger blocks are required. A wire passing round a block generates considerable internal friction in the wire which can wear away the wire strands, particularly if there are any tiny particles of grit in the wire. The minimum diameter of block sheave which should be considered is 10 times the diameter of the wire and preferably 12 times.

Oiling wires can extend their life considerably. Not only does the oil reduce corrosion but also helps to lubricate the strands. A fish oil is generally used for the purpose as it does not harm the fibres incorporated in a lay-up of the wire. There are also special oils on the market for the purpose and these have the benefit of not being easily washed away by water.

Trawl wires are expensive and it is surprising that fishermen do not pay more attention to handling them carefully. Blocks are generally badly maintained and too small in diameter. One often sees grooves worn into the sheaves on trawlers, so obviously the sheave is not turning freely. Once there is this unevenness in the surface of the sheave wear on the wire is even more rapid.

The many blocks and lead rollers used on a fishing boat have a hard life. They are continually soaked in salt water and are subjected to abrasive grit brought on board with the trawl. Regular greasing of the pins and swivels can help to maintain them in good condition and so allow the wires to run smoothly.

Considerable wear and tear can be caused to ropes of all types by mishandling in one way or another. Time and effort spent in arranging them correctly in the first place, combined with care and attention in using them, can help to prolong the life of the ropes, and at the same time it will greatly reduce the chances of an accident.

CHAPTER 11

Electronics and Navigation Equipment

Modern electronics present the fisherman with a bewildering choice. The electronics on a fishing boat can represent a sixth of the total cost of the boat and with continuing developments in this field, this figure could well increase in the future. The problem is how to make a choice from the vast array of equipment available. Much will depend on the type of fishing being carried out, but apart from this there are many basic principles which should be understood.

Most fishing boats now carry a radio. The benefits are communications with the shore for routine arrival or departure information, a means of summoning help in emergencies and of obtaining weather forecasts and talking to other craft in the fishing area. The very high frequency (VHF) radio which has come into almost universal use over the last ten years is used a great deal, particularly for inshore boats.

VHF radio is limited in range to more or less line of sight from aerial to aerial but this is adequate for many practical purposes. For maximum range the aerial on the boat should be placed as high as possible. The sets are compact, easy to install and operate, and have brought a new dimension to communications at sea. For many fishing boats a VHF installation is now a compulsory fitting in some countries and this may extend to all fishing boats in the not too distant future. The benefits of VHF radio far outweigh the cost and should therefore be considered essential.

The VHF radio has largely replaced the medium frequency (MF) for short range work, but where boats are working some distance from the shore the MF radio is the best way to maintain communications. The cost of these sets has increased recently now the simpler double sideband (DSB) equipment is no longer permitted, and fishing boats have to install the single sideband (SSB) equipment. An SSB radio is quite a large piece of equipment and it is not always easy to find room for it in the confines of a small boat wheelhouse. Several manufacturers have sought solutions to this problem and there should be a marked reduction in size and an increase in reliability as smaller sets become available.

The SSB MF radios rely on crystal tuning for both the transmitter and the receiver and this restricts the selection of frequencies. This is usually no problem on the transmission side where the frequencies are selected to suit the area of use, but for reception it can restrict the ability to receive weather forecasts. A separate receiver is often carried for this purpose. This receiver can also be used to receive normal radio broadcasts and may be wired to extension speakers in other parts of the boat.

On VHF, channel 16 is the calling and distress frequency and on MF, 2182 kHz provides the same function. Radio equipped vessels are expected to monitor these frequencies so that distress calls do not go unheeded. Many VHF radios are fitted with a dual watch facility so that channel 16 is monitored regardless of which other frequency is being used. On MF a separate fixed frequency watch receiver is a compulsory fitting on some boats, not only to monitor 2182 kHz, but also to sound an alarm if a distress signal is heard.

The aerial used for VHF sets is usually a dipole, which is in effect two metal rods each about 2 feet long encased in a GRP housing. This is light and easy to mount. For MF radios the aerial can be either a copper wire strung between the masts or, as is now more commonly fitted, a whip aerial mounted on the wheelhouse top.

Radio installations on board boats are covered by international regulations which demand high standards and they must be licensed, as well as the people who operate them. The latter have to pass a simple test in operating procedures largely to ensure that some sort of discipline is exercised over the use of radios. It was lack of discipline which led to the introduction of watch receivers. It is intended that all countries will enforce the requirement for fishing boats over 40 feet long to be fitted with an SSB MF radio in due course, and there are likely to be major changes in the frequencies which can be used.

Radar sets must be licensed in the same way as radios because they are transmitters, but this is a formality. A much more difficult problem facing fishing boat owners is whether the cost of a radar set is justified, and if so, which type to choose.

Radar has been regarded as one of the major innovations of the modern world, and by presenting a picture of what is going on around a vessel at sea, both fixed objects such as the land and moving objects such as other craft, it comes close to the ideal navigation instrument. There are two main functions of radar, one is its use for navigation, where it competes with other position finding equipment, and the other is its use for collision avoidance where it has little competition.

Radar is not much use for fishing operations, although it can help prevent collisions if the visibility is bad. It can also be useful for locating dan buoys marking pots and nets if these are fitted with a radar reflector. Radar can be used for position finding on inshore fishing grounds, but the method is cumbersome compared with other systems and does not always have the degree of accuracy required.

The chief use of radar is to provide safety in getting to and from the fishing grounds under all weather conditions. Other position finding systems can indicate whether the correct course is being followed but they are of limited use in entering or leaving harbour in poor visibility and they cannot indicate other vessels which are in the vicinity. The justification for installing a radar set is the ability to take a boat to sea almost irrespective of the prevailing visibility, so that fishing ability is largely dictated only by sea conditions.

The difference between profit and loss on fishing operations can be small enough at the best of times, and the ability to gain the extra ten or twenty days a year when visibility is bad can make a great deal of difference to profit. The difference becomes greater as the size of boat increases; it costs much more for a larger boat to be tied up in harbour than a small boat yet there is little difference in the price of a suitable radar set.

There are many good small boat radar sets available, all of which have the same basic features. Choice usually has to be made in terms of maximum range, size of plan position indicator (PPI) and the various options offered. How does the fisherman know that he is getting something worthwhile if he pays extra?

Maximum range is not critical for fishing boats. A range of 24 miles is quite adequate because other position finding equipment can be used away from land. The prime need is for a radar which will help in navigating in and out of harbour and to prevent collisions. Good discrimination is needed, which means the largest possible scanner (a point often overlooked) and also the largest possible plan position indicator is required so that a clear picture is obtained. Both for collision avoidance and for close quarters navigation a variable range marker is a great help, both for accurate navigation and to determine the movements of other vessels.

In general terms, the radar should be simple to operate and install and, as far as possible, it should be proof against damp conditions. The ease with which a radar set can be operated depends a great deal on how it is installed. This has been discussed briefly in Chapter 9. It is best fitted so that the observer is looking down into the PPI, and he should be facing forward. This helps when the equipment has to be used in rough seas and assists the user to orientate himself correctly.

Strong hand holds are required so that the observer can position himself against the movement of the boat and there should be somewhere to spread a chart out alongside the radar for comparison purposes.

Obtaining the right radar set and installing it correctly are only part of the problem. The information presented by the radar looks so clear and obvious. However, it will only make sense if it is interpreted properly, and this requires practice. It is very easy to make false assumptions about the echoes seen on the radar screen, and only constant use will enable the observer to make best use of the equipment, particularly when visibility is very poor and he is relying completely on the radar.

Courses are available for training in the use of radar, but the best method, after a basic grounding, is constant practice, using the radar to navigate in clear weather. Only then will the observer have sufficient confidence when conditions are bad.

Some very small radar sets are being produced which are inexpensive. They have a very limited range and lack much of the sophistication of the larger sets, but provided that one is aware of the limitations of these sets, they can provide useful information. By appearing to present all the answers when in the middle of a thick fog, radar can give a great feeling of confidence. It is over-confidence in its use which causes radar to lead many people into trouble.

The value of radar for the larger fishing boat is emphasized by the increasing number of craft fitting two radar sets. There are two purposes in fitting twin sets, one being to ensure that the vessel is never without radar even in the event of the failure of one set, and the second being that it offers the opportunity to have two sets with different characteristics to meet particular conditions. Some radars are specifically designed for use in confined waters while others are designed for anti-collision work. Having two radars means that less compromise has to be made with the conflicting factors involved in radar design.

While radar can provide a degree of position finding information, most fishing boats require more precise information, and for this they tend to rely on hyperbolic navigation systems. The two main systems are Decca Navigator and Loran. These can provide positions with a good degree of accuracy even well away from land, but even more important, they have a very high level of repeatability, enabling a vessel to return to a previously determined position with great accuracy. This is very useful for finding strings of pots or for avoiding wrecks and snags when trawling.

Decca Navigator is a system whose coverage extends over most of the Northern European waters and has been extended to some Mediterranean and Persian Gulf and United States waters. Transmis-

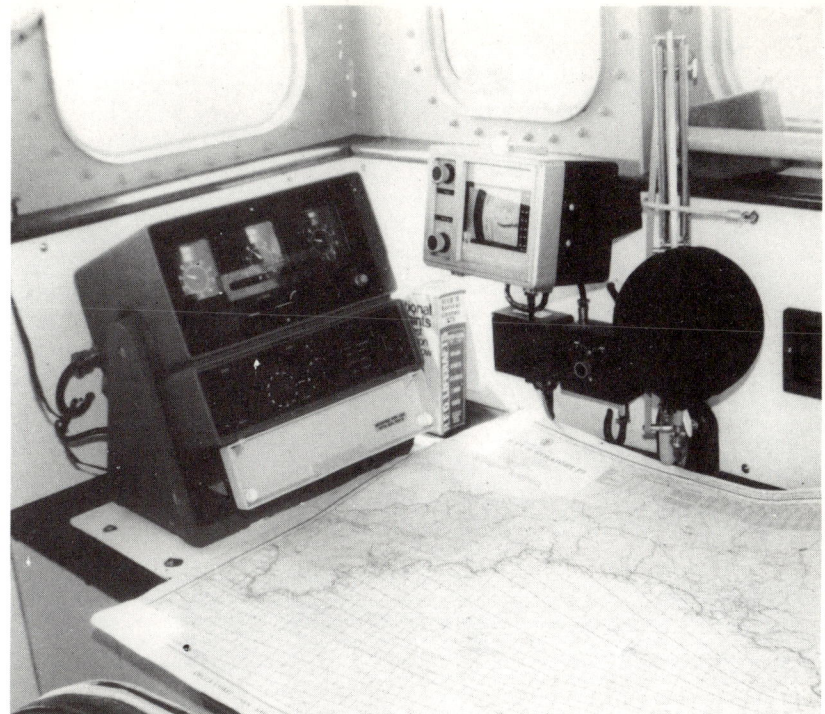

Fig 57   A Decca Navigator installation with the special chart which has to be used with this equipment.

sions are made from a pattern of four shore-based stations, one master and three slave stations. The position is found by measuring the phase difference between the signals from the master and two or more of the slave stations. These give a numerical read out on appropriate coloured dials which can be related to numbered coloured lines overprinted on standard navigation charts. The position is indicated by the point where two lines cross, although allowance may have to be made for certain corrections if a high degree of accuracy is required.

Accuracy depends a great deal on the angle at which the position lines cross and in good areas it can be within 100 feet (30 m). The accuracy diminishes as distance from the transmitting stations increases up to a maximum range of around 400 miles. For the small boat working coastal waters Decca Navigator is very useful. Fitting this equipment does not add to the capital cost of a boat as it can be rented, the rentals helping to meet the cost of running the transmitting stations.

145

Loran is a system somewhat similar to the Decca Navigator and is available in two versions. Loran A, the first system to be introduced, established lines of position by measuring the time difference between signals from the master and slave stations. It had a much greater range than Decca Navigator, being effective up to 1,500 miles from the transmitting stations, but the accuracy at close ranges was not as good and it decreased considerably as distance from the station increased.

The sets installed for receiving Loran A required a degree of skill on the part of the operator in recognizing and watching the incoming signals on the cathode ray tube. Later a more sophisticated version of the system was introduced called Loran C, which was virtually automatic in operation and displayed the position line numbers as a digital read out, so that all that was required was plotting. Loran C found the position line by measuring both the time and phase difference between the signals and thus was able to achieve a degree of accuracy comparable to the Decca Navigator with a longer range capability.

The Loran systems are operated by the US Government and all that is required to use the system is to buy or lease a receiving set. A great

Fig 58   A manual Loran receiver which can be used on both the A and C systems.

Fig 59 A Loran position plotter which has a small computer incorporated to give an undistorted plot.

number of these sets are in production by many of the major electronics firms, some sets able to receive both Loran A and C. This is to cover the period of change-over between the two systems. At present Loran A covers much of the northern hemisphere, certainly as far as the Atlantic coasts are concerned. New Loran C stations are being established and it is planned to have the US coasts covered by 1980 and European coasts a little later.

Both Decca and Loran C can be automated one stage further by the use of a track plotter. This is a device where the output from the receivers is used to control a moving pen which can draw a permanent record of the track followed. This enables special charts to be made up of selected fishing areas, and each fisherman can keep his own record of where he has fished and areas where there are rocks or wrecks likely to snag a trawl.

Decca and Loran are in widespread use in fishing boats and are regarded by many fishermen as being indispensable. The information they give enables fishing to be carried out in a much more controlled manner with considerable savings in terms of effort and damage to gear, which more than offsets the costs of the equipment.

Two other electronic navigation systems are in use in large fishing boats but have little application for the smaller boat. These are Omega, which is a worldwide hyperbolic system, and satellite navigation which uses signals from a special series of satellites. The accuracy of the latter can be quite high, but Omega only gives positions to an accuracy of 1 or 2 miles which is satisfactory for ocean navigation but not for coastal fishing.

Hyperbolic navigation systems used in conjunction with fish finding equipment form the basis of the equipment on most fishing boats. The growth in the use and the complexity of electronics for detecting fish has been one of the major revolutions in fishing, and there is now a very wide range of equipment from which to choose, making it difficult for the fisherman to gauge the requirements for his particular boat. One way is to allocate a certain amount of money for fish finding equipment and then spend up to this level. Careful choice of the equipment can mean, however, that if the right basic units are bought it will be possible to extend the capabilities at a later date.

Fig 60 A combination of navigation systems. On the left is a Loran C receiver, in the centre a Decca Navigator, top right is an Omega receiver and on the bottom right is an automatic radio direction finder. It is unusual to find all these together but two or more might be found on one vessel.

Fish finding equipment is in three basic forms. There are sets which will search the area immediately under the boat, working in the same way as an echo sounder. This device sends a sound beam down which is reflected back from the sea bed or from fish. There is an obvious limitation in the use of this equipment in that it is necessary to pass right over the fish to find them.

A more sophisticated type of fish finder is the searching sonar, where the sound beam can be directed in any desired direction around the vessel to search out shoals of fish. On sophisticated equipment the angle of tilt of the beam can be altered as well, so that it is possible to pinpoint a shoal closely.

Here the third type of equipment becomes useful. A transducer which transmits sound waves is attached to the net or trawl so that it is possible to adjust the trawl to the same depth as the fish. By this means much of the guesswork is taken out of fishing and the results achieved demonstrate the effectiveness of such equipment.

Let us consider the first type of fish finder which only scans the area directly under the boat. Many manufacturers of simple navigation echo sounders claim that their equipment is capable of detecting fish. This may be possible with extremely dense shoals of fish, but in general this type of equipment, which displays its readings either on illuminated dials or on a paper recorder, is only suited for general navigation. Echo sounders of this type are relatively cheap and can be very useful in poor visibility when close to the coast. However, they cannot be expected to do the work of the sophisticated fish finding equipment.

The fish finder uses the same technique as the echo sounder, but the emphasis in the design is to detect and display the weak echoes received from fish rather than the bottom echoes. Much more power is used in the signal than with an ordinary echo sounder, and it is frequently possible to vary the frequency of the signal. This latter facility, together with the ability to vary the pulse length, makes it possible to select the optimum settings to suit the type of fish being located and the depth of the water.

Most manufacturers produce a range of models which can be adapted for different fishing requirements. They can operate to different maximum depths. There is the facility to select just a portion of the scale and expand this to obtain a clearer indication of fish. For bottom trawling it is possible to have the set automatically displaying the area just above the sea bed with a clear space separating the sea bed from any fish echoes just above it.

To give a clear indication of fish echoes, a cathode ray tube display is often added to the echo sounder. This allows specific areas of the display to be expanded at will, while the paper recorder is showing the general pattern.

The searching sonar uses a display similar to the echo sounder type with

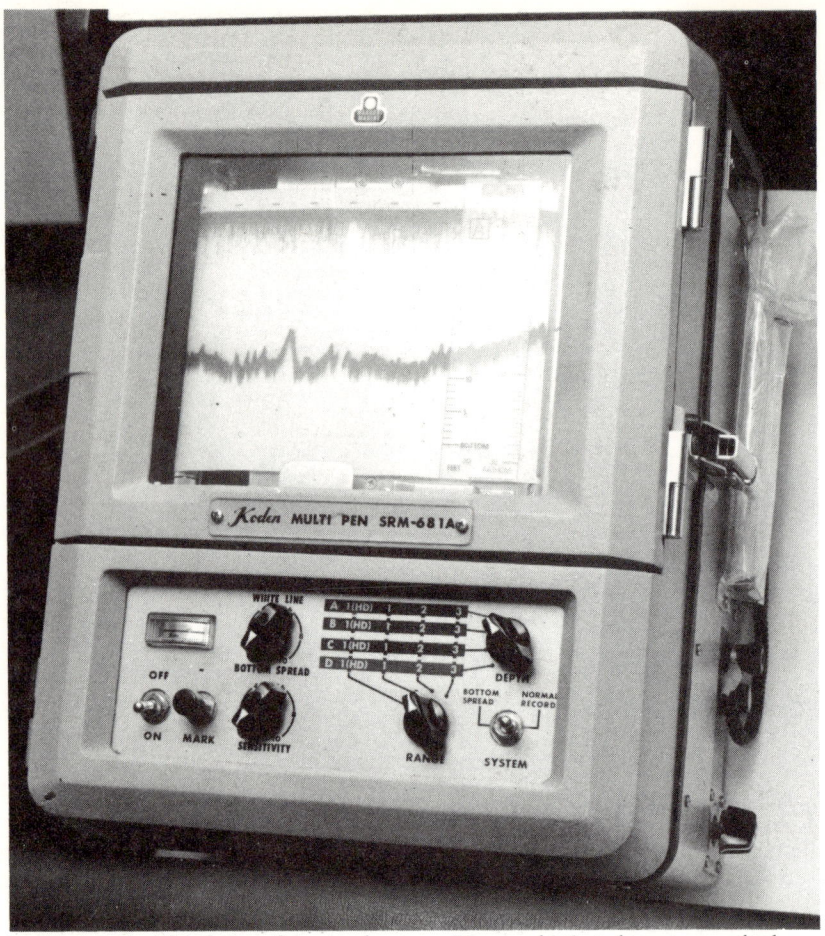

Fig 61 A typical fish finder of the simplest type. More sophisticated types use cathode ray tubes for the presentation.

additional information showing the direction and angle of tilt of the transducer. The principle is the same: a sound signal is sent out by the transducer which is reflected by anything in its path, be it the sea bed or a shoal of fish, and the result is indicated on paper by a pen. Particularly useful with the sonar is a cathode ray tube (CRT) which gives, in effect, a plan view of the area being searched, rather like an underwater radar. This makes it much easier to orientate the shoal when it is located.

The range of these searching sonars can be up to 2 miles, but fish detection is much more positive at closer ranges. There are more simple sets available with a smaller range using only a CRT display, but these sets cannot be expected to give the same results as the more sophisticated equipment.

The key part of an echo sounder or a sonar is the transducer which transmits and receives the sound waves. For an echo sounder or fixed fish finder, the transducer is either attached to the outside of the hull or a through hull fastening is used. Simple navigation echo sounders use a transducer which may be only an inch in diameter and the same transducer both transmits and receives.

Fish finding echo sounders may use one or two transducers. Where two are used there is less compromise because each transducer is designed for its particular function, one to transmit and one to receive. To work satisfactorily, transducers must be very carefully located on the hull and carefully installed so that there is a good flow of water around and across them. The transducer usually stands proud of the hull to reduce the size of the hole through the hull and so it must be faired in with wooden blocks to smooth out the flow of water.

When installing a transducer it is necessary to prevent the formation of air bubbles in its vicinity during passage through the water. Air bubbles in the sound beam will produce a strong reflection, and these can prevent any meaningful readings being recorded. As air bubbles can be produced by the forward motion of the boat which forces air under the boat, the normal position of the transducers is just aft of amidships and close to the keel. There is less possibility of a good installation on a small boat where air bubbles are much more prevalent, particularly in a rough sea when the boat is pitching heavily. Little can be done about this except to moderate the speed.

The transducer should not be too close to the propeller because this will create stray noises which might affect the readings. Readings should not be taken when going astern as the propeller will drive air bubbles along the hull from the stern.

The transducer on searching sonars is much more complex but the same installation principles apply. If the boat is fitted with an outside keel, then obviously the transducer must project below this otherwise one side will be obscured. A typical transducer will be spherical, about a foot (30 cm) in diameter and mounted on a stem. This stem allows the transducer to be raised and lowered and swung around. A separate control inside the spindle adjusts the elevation of the transducer. The transducer is totally enclosed in a plastic sphere, and the whole apparatus can be withdrawn into a compartment in the bilges so that it will not be damaged when the boat is slipped or takes the bottom. The raising or lowering of the apparatus is done by means of switches on the recorder in the wheelhouse.

The manufacturers of sounders and sonars have much experience in installing their equipment, and it is well to discuss particular requirements with them at the design stage of the boat, so that the necessary features can be incorporated into the hull. It is not so easy to add essential features once the hull is built, particularly if it is a sonar which is being fitted. There is always a problem in trying to keep a boat up to date during the twenty or so years of its life, and with the continued improvements being made in this equipment, several changes may be required during the life of the boat.

Manufacturers are generally aware of this problem and try to standardize as much as possible, with most of the improvements being made in the wheelhouse area. One of the most recent improvements is a colour cathode ray tube display which, it is claimed, will provide even clearer definition between fish and other echoes. The manufacturers claim that even different types of fish can be identified. It is improvements like this which show the need to have space available for future developments.

The use of portable transducers which can be mounted on the trawl itself has been largely responsible for the development of mid-water trawling. The simplest form of these transducers has only one element pointing downwards, which is used to measure the height of the trawl off the sea bed, and it also indicates the opening of the trawl by picking up reflections from the foot rope.

More sophisticated units have multiple elements which can measure the depth of the shoal below the surface and can also locate any fish approaching the trawl. This equipment gives a complete picture of how the trawl is behaving as well as giving an indication of the amount of fish being caught. It can also reveal problems that may arise with the trawl.

The transducer is connected to the boat by means of a specially protected co-axial cable which is normally reeled in or fed out automatically, so that a steady strain is kept on the cable. The reels used for this cable can be either electrically or hydraulically driven. The information from these net transducers can be shown on a paper recorder and indeed, the normal fish finder can be switched over for this purpose, but it is normal to have a separate recorder.

In mid-water trawling the height of the trawl is adjusted by varying the speed of the boat. A skipper may judge this by experience, but a log is often fitted as a guide. Modern logs are small and unobtrusive compared with the older types which were towed astern, and they are comparatively inexpensive, comparable in price to the most inexpensive echo sounders.

There are several types of speed measuring devices, each employing a transducer mounted in the bottom of the boat. One of the simplest is that with a pitot tube which is open at its forward end to the water flowing past the boat. The speed is measured by the variation of the pressure in the tube, but this type is not very sensitive and the movement of a small boat in a heavy sea can produce wild fluctuations.

Another type uses a small impeller projecting below the bottom of the boat. The movement of the hull through the water causes the impeller to rotate and a magnetic pick-up counts the revolutions and translates these to distance and speed. Both types have the disadvantage of projections below the bottom of the boat which are liable to damage either by the fishing gear or by debris floating in the water.

A third type has a flush mounted transducer with two electrodes. The current induced in these electrodes by the water flowing past is a function of the speed. The simplicity of this electromagnetic log has to be offset against possible unreliable readings due to uneven flow along the boundary layers of the hull, but in general this equipment works well if the transducer is carefully sited.

The fourth type is the Doppler log which is based on the change in frequency of a reflected sound signal. The frequency change is related to the speed, and one advantage of this type of log is that it can indicate speed relative to the sea bed rather than speed through the water, a useful feature when bottom trawling. However, unless the equipment is fairly sophisticated, which also means expensive, it will only give readings from the bottom up to a certain depth, possibly 40 fathoms, depending on the equipment. Below this depth the readings are taken from particles suspended in the water which, of course, only indicate the speed through the water.

Doppler logs are likely to improve in the future and the information provided could be useful to fishermen, particularly as fishing becomes more and more complex.

All this equipment — fish finders, echo sounders and logs which use underwater transducers — rely heavily on a clean face to the transducer to give good readings. These should never be painted when the hull is treated with anti-fouling material, and marine growth should be very carefully removed — preferably with a wooden scraper. This can be usefully done by a diver between the periods when the boat is slipped.

Insufficient thought seems to be given to the fitting of compasses to fishing boats. Once the skipper has surrounded himself with a mass of electronic equipment (all of which can affect the readings of the compass) space must be found for the compass. This is why the compass is frequently mounted on top of the wheelhouse and the readings shown in the wheelhouse by means of mirrors.

Much development has taken place in magnetic compasses over the past few years, largely as a result of the increase in small boating in general, and compasses are now available which are much better suited to the often violent movements of small boats. A compass mounted in gimbals will often accentuate the motion of a small boat because the inertia in the compass bowl causes it to over-react to the movement.

Modern compasses have the card mounted in a spherical bowl so that only the light card moves in response to the movement of the boat, and readings are much steadier. The bowl is filled with a damping liquid which can be given different characteristics to suit different boats. A fast boat will need heavier damping than a slower boat and the compass should be selected accordingly.

Even with these compasses there can still be considerable card movement in rough seas. There is a modern magnetic compass which senses the earth's magnetic field electronically. This gives very steady readings which can be displayed either as a standard compass card, as a course pointer or by digits. One of the main advantages of this type of compass is that the detection unit can be mounted in a position where there is little magnetic influence and the readings displayed remotely. This still means that the compass must be corrected, as with the ordinary type of compass, but there is more likelihood of obtaining reliable readings as the variable compass influences will have been removed.

A third type of compass now being used to an increasing extent on larger fishing boats is the gyro compass. This compass is entirely free from magnetic influence and gives reliable readings of true directions. The corrections required are fed into the controls and no allowance for deviation or variation is necessary. Cost is the main objection to this type of compass, and because it requires an electrical supply, a magnetic compass is still required as a standby. Modern types of gyro compass have many of the mechanical parts replaced by electronics which provide greater reliability and reduces both the size and cost of the equipment.

All three types of compass can be used as a direction source for an auto-pilot. Because of their steadier readings the electronic and gyro compasses are preferable to the standard magnetic compass, but the magnetic compass is less costly.

The auto-pilot can offer many advantages, the most obvious being the saving in manpower because no-one is required to be at the wheel the whole time. This allows the person on watch to carry out routine navigation duties. When fishing single handed a steady course can be maintained with an auto-pilot, which permits concentration on the other controls and equipment. By steering steady courses fuel can be

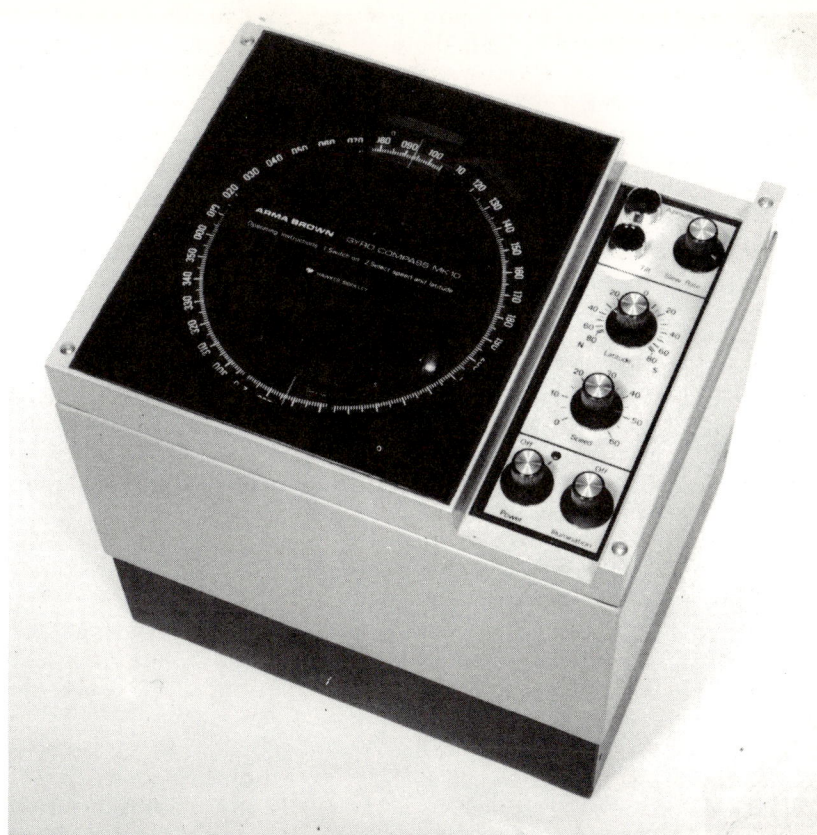

Fig 62 A gyro compass suitable for fitting to medium and large sized fishing boats. The adjustments only require slight attention and steering is usually by means of repeaters.

saved. Estimates vary, but even at a conservative 1%, this saving can, over some years, more than cover the cost of the auto-pilot.

The benefits of the auto-pilot are not confined to more efficient course steering. The system, with its power steering, lends itself to remote control being fitted, and this can be carried about the deck on the end of an extension cable if required. For potters, where the steering control is often required at the hauling position, this is easy to arrange.

Auto-pilots for smaller boats are usually provided as a complete kit. The steering signals from the compass sensor unit are fed to a reversible electric motor which connects by chain to the steering wheel.

155

Larger boats will often have a power steering system fitted, usually of the electric/hydraulic type and the auto-pilot is arranged to connect into this.

Alarms are essential in the system and the simplest one indicates when the boat has strayed more than a set number of degrees off the selected course. This will cover all such problems as mechanical and electrical failures which can cause the boat to wander off course. However, the alarm does not solve all the problems, as there is still the need to keep a good look out. The auto-pilot may keep the boat on course, but it cannot ensure that the projected course is clear.

This survey covers the main electronic equipment used on board fishing boats, but there are several other pieces of equipment which may be used, and the list is likely to grow in the future. There is unlikely to be any interaction between the various items except for the space available to fit them, and also the aerials. Radios, radar and the hyperbolic navigation systems all require aerials, and these should be kept as far apart as possible, particularly the main radio transmitting aerial which can radiate a fair amount of power.

Television sets are being fitted on fishing boats and the aerial requirements can be critical for good reception. Special non-directional aerials are available for use on boats and these should be mounted as high as possible to avoid any interference. Television sets normally require a mains voltage supply, but there are now small portable sets available which can work off internal batteries or a 12 or 24 volt supply.

Electronics are used in the gas detectors required when a gas cooking or heating system is installed. The gas sensor is mounted in the lowest part of the compartment or in the bilges, and if gas is present it can give an audio or visual warning. More complex equipment is available which also detects water in the bilges and the alarm signal can be used to switch on electric bilge pumps or fans to clear the water or gas. Because an explosive gas mixture could be present in the engine compartment, the starting switch can be interconnected so that the engine cannot be started until the gas has been cleared. Each compartment, where there is a possibility of gas accumulating, should have its own sensor.

Communications about the boat can be provided by an intercom system. These can be by means of a telephone system internally and a loud speaker talk back system for external stations on deck. As wheelhouses become more enclosed, these provide means of communications between wheelhouse and deck.

The use of electronics on board fishing boats has increased considerably over the past few years and this trend is likely to continue. As designers of electronic equipment become more skilled in concentrating the most complex equipment into a small case, so it is likely that even small fishing boats may start using such equipment. The deciding factor will be cost. How much more fish can be caught by using more sophisticated navigation and detection equipment? If the cost of electronic equipment is to be justified, then it must be costed carefully with the potential increase in catches.

CHAPTER 12

Secondhand Fishing Boats

Many fishermen purchase a secondhand vessel, for various reasons. The attraction may be the lower cost than that of a new boat or the fact that the boat is readily available and there is no waiting for it to be built. Most fishing magazines carry advertisements for secondhand fishing boats, and there are many reputable brokers who specialize in these craft.

When the decision has been made to buy a secondhand vessel, it is as well to specify exactly the requirements. There may be a preference for a particular construction material, or size and type of engine. The deck layout and other factors should be carefully considered.

Price will be a limiting factor and this must be decided beforehand, bearing in mind what may have to be spent on the boat to bring it up to the required standard. A cheap boat may need a great deal of money to be spent on it before it is fit to fish. To spend all the available money on acquiring the boat and have little or nothing left for repairs or modifications is a false economy and dangerous.

Looking over secondhand boats can be expensive in time and money, therefore as much information as possible should be obtained beforehand. Photographs should be requested, because appearance will be one of the major factors affecting a decision, but this will not indicate the condition of a boat.

Before coming to any decision it is as well to look at several boats. This gives a better idea of what is available for the price and an appreciation of the one finally decided upon. Boats are often bought without the prospective owner having a trial run, but this is something which should be insisted upon. A trial run can reveal all sorts of snags and irritations which may not otherwise be apparent.

A trial run also shows how the machinery is behaving. This should be surveyed by a qualified engineer, but one of the best indications of the condition of an engine is the way the outside has been maintained. External corrosion, patched and repaired pipework and leaking fuel lines all indicate that the engine has not been receiving its fair share of attention. There is no excuse for the engine compartment of a fishing boat to be dirty, and lack of application to this item must reflect on the general standards of maintenance.

If the trial run and the general appearance of the boat prove satisfactory then the next stage is to check the condition of the boat. This requires money to be spent on surveyor's fees, but a preliminary examination should be made by the prospective owner. As far as possible, look into all the hidden corners of the boat such as the bow, stern and bilges.

On wooden boats any decay will show up as soft wood which can be detected by prodding with a screwdriver. Corrosion or wasting on a steel boat is an indication that all is not well and the same can apply to a ferro-cement hull. On GRP hulls discolouration and cracks are the main indicators of a defect.

If the decay or corrosion is extensive then it may be preferable to look for another boat. It may not be worth paying the surveyor's fees only to be told what is already suspected. On the other hand, a surveyor's job is not only to find the areas where there are problems, but also to assess the extent of the decay and to find out how much it is affecting the strength and safety of the boat.

If a particular boat is being seriously considered, then a surveyor's report should be obtained. If the report only confirms what the prospective owner suspects then this is reassuring; if it brings to light some extensive hidden defects then it can save a great deal of money.

Employing a surveyor does mean the outlay of money, so before this point is reached it is as well to negotiate a sale price with the owner. The price of most secondhand boats is negotiable and worthwhile savings can often be made. The price agreed should always be stated as being 'subject to survey'. This leaves room for a further negotiation of the price in the event of undeclared defects coming to light in the survey report or to the cancelling of the sale if the survey report is really adverse.

Try to find a surveyor who is experienced in the class of vessel which is being bought. A yacht surveyor will not necessarily be aware of the problems affecting fishing boats and the standards required, so a few pertinent questions about the surveyor's experience and qualifications are warranted. An experienced surveyor will not object to them.

A survey is only worthwhile if the boat is out of the water. A survey conducted with the boat afloat means that half the hull of the boat is not visible for inspection and this is the most important part. The cost involved in drying the boat out or hauling it up a slipway will normally fall on the prospective owner, but many vendors are happy to accept this as part of the cost of selling the boat. It is a point to check with the owner when arranging for a survey to be carried out.

A surveyor can only report on what he can see. Many parts of the inside of the hull can only be seen after removing linings or floors. It is not part of the surveyor's job to do this and if these are to be examined then arrange with the owner to have this work done.

A surveyor's report will be useful in other ways. Many insurance companies demand a survey report before insuring older vessels and a bank may require a report before lending money on the vessel. The surveyor's report can also provide a useful guide to the work which must be done on the vessel to bring it up to standard.

The extent to which an older boat requires refitting will depend a great deal on the treatment it has received during its life and the future use intended for the vessel. On reasonably sound boats, in terms of hull and engine condition it will probably be sufficient to check thoroughly the piping and wiring systems, to be assured that it will last for many years.

If the boat was soundly built, it may be the deck gear and wheel-house which show the main deterioration. Sturdily built fishing boat hulls will often remain in sound condition when the fittings and fix-tures are deteriorating. By buying an old boat and completely refitting it, it is often possible to obtain a fishing vessel which will give a good many years of service at must less than the cost of a new vessel.

By replacing rotted timbers and planking in a wooden hull and cor-roded steel in a metal hull, the hull can be brought up to a nearly new condition as far as durability is concerned. To do this may mean strip-ping the hull down to bare essentials which can involve much work. If this is undertaken it is probably wise to renew wiring and piping.

Removing the engine to gain access to the hull provides a good opportunity for a complete overhaul. This, together with the work on the hull and ancillaries, leads to a boat which should render good ser-vice for many years. The initial cost may be fairly high, but it should be well below the cost of a new boat, and there are unlikely to be any major expenses for several years if the work is done properly.

When carrying out such an overhaul do not forget the stern gear, the most neglected area on fishing boats. With the boat stripped out, work on the stern tube and shaft and the rudder is comparatively sim-ple. Maintenance work in this area is never wasted and can provide peace of mind when at sea.

One of the likely problems with an older boat is that less attention was paid to space on deck and in the fish hold when the design was made. These factors are more critical in modern fishing operations and a complete refit can be the time to gain more space.

Greater deck space can be achieved by moving the wheelhouse for-ward and merging it into a raised forecastle. This is a fairly major reconstruction job because it is not just a matter of reconstructing the superstructure. Much of the electric wiring will have to be altered and new engine controls and other fittings will add considerably to the cost.

Gaining extra space in the fish hold may be even more difficult because it usually entails moving bulkheads. If these were watertight, they are probably an integral part of the hull structure, but on many old boats the bulkheads are simply a wooden partition. If this is the case, space may be found at the expense of the engine room or the accommodation, and in fitting new bulkheads it is as well to consider making these watertight and, if they adjoin the engine, fireproof as well.

In time, the cost advantages of refitting an old boat as opposed to buying a new vessel may be lost or at least eroded. The future is likely to bring increasing legislation governing the construction of fishing vessels to ensure greater safety. These legislation requirements are relatively easy to design into new boats, but are likely to become increasingly difficult to incorporate into older vessels, particularly where structural alterations are required. The main problems likely to be encountered are the openings in the deck and superstructure and fireproofing arrangements.

Other problems likely to arise on older fishing boats are in adapting the vessel to modern fishing methods. The increasing use of deck machinery can take up valuable deck space, and the power required to operate the machinery may take considerable part of the engine power. One solution may be to fit an auxiliary engine to supply part or all of this additional demand load. It could also supply additional electrical power, which is often a problem on older boats.

The increasing use of electronics on fishing boats poses problems in terms of wheelhouse space and design. This equipment must be kept dry and some of the wheelhouses on older boats are not noted for their watertightness. The physical size of modern electrical equipment is decreasing, but there must be sufficient room for it to be used and operated efficiently.

Buying a secondhand fishing boat is the way in which the majority of fishermen begin their independent career. By analysing the requirements beforehand and being cautious, there is no reason why a secondhand boat should not give many years of satisfactory service. It may be more difficult in later years to maintain the vessels to the standards required by legislation, but this is likely to have the effect of reducing the price of secondhand vessels relative to that of new vessels so that more expense can be justified in bringing the vessels up to standard.

CHAPTER 13

Maintenance

Immediately after a fishing boat has been completed it starts to deteriorate; in fact it is probably deteriorating even before it is completed. Careful maintenance can arrest this deterioration in many parts but however much care is taken it can never be eliminated completely. For this reason, a good fishing boat is built with a considerable reserve of strength so that the losses due to wear and tear will not soon make it unseaworthy.

The amount and quality of the maintenance carried out on a fishing boat will be largely determined by the way the boat has been put together. Maintenance can only be given to areas that can be reached, so that all the hidden corners are likely to be neglected until some serious fault develops. Careful thought at the design stage can eliminate many of the problems of maintenance.

On the outside of the hull access is simple when the boat is out of the water, and maintenance can usually be restricted to slipping the boat annually for renewing the anti-fouling. In areas where marine growth is bad, then slipping twice a year, once in the late spring and once in the autumn, may be worthwhile, because the build-up of marine growth will affect both speed and fuel consumption, as well as reducing the water flow in the engine and stern tube cooling inlets.

When the boat is out of the water all the stern gear must be very thoroughly examined for wear and tear. Any wear in the rudder or stern tube bearings will increase rapidly. This will lead to the boat being taken out of service at short notice, probably just when the fishing is particularly good. If the original design allows the rudder and aft stern tube bearings to be renewed easily, it would be good practice to renew these when the boat is slipped. By so doing, the skipper can be confident that all is well under the water.

The same attitude can be taken with fittings such as the zinc anodes fitted to reduce the effects of electrolytic action between the propeller and other metal fittings. Do not think that because they are only half

162

eroded away, they will last for another year. They may disappear completely before the boat is next slipped and allow corrosion to start.

Work on the hull itself will depend much on both its condition and the material from which it is made. The maintenance of steel and wood are fairly well understood, but GRP and ferro-cement are less familiar to fishermen and are often presented as maintenance-free materials. The actual methods used will be discussed later, but suffice to say here, that design can simplify the maintenance. Where timber strips have to be fitted to protect a GRP or ferro-cement hull from chafing by the fishing gear, these should be fitted as a continuous piece. This timber has to be painted and the intricate painting of a whole series of strips can be more time consuming than painting the whole of the hull.

Access to the interior of the hull can be difficult. Linings placed in the fish hold and in the accommodation can make it impossible to gain access to the side of the boat. Fuel tanks placed at the side of the engine can have the same effect, and here there may be deterioration of both the tank and the framing and planking. These areas are probably only examined when the boat is surveyed and then the surveyor may be reluctant to rip out linings to see what is happening behind.

It says much for the original construction of fishing boats that they can stand up to this neglect. On wooden boats the timber is usually treated with a preservative such as Cuprinol which can help a great deal in preventing rot, but this must be applied carefully to all the surfaces exposed during construction if it is to be effective. Areas around bolt holes are particularly vulnerable and are often the place where rot starts.

On steel boats the initial preparation of the inside of the hull is even more important. If the hull is carefully sand-blasted when completed and then coated with one of the modern epoxy paints, corrosion will be kept at bay for a long time. Corrosion starts when the hull is being fitted out, because this protective skin is broken by drilling holes for fastenings or welding on fittings.

On and around the deck and fishing gear maintenance costs can be reduced and the task simplified if the problems are thought out at the design stage. Any pocket where water can collect on deck will be a source of possible rot or corrosion, so a designer should take particular care to obtain a good water flow off the deck. Drains and scuppers must be carefully positioned allowing for changes in trim of the boat.

Wear will take place between any two parts which rub together. If this cannot be avoided then they should be provided with a positive means of lubrication to reduce the wear or at least reduce it to controllable limits. Grease nipples are usually fitted to the most important

Fig 63 Wear comes in unusual places. This chain looks fairly sound until the links are opened up.

bearing surfaces such as those in the blocks and winches, but this alone is not enough. Quite often the nipples are badly placed, and in the rough and tumble of handling fishing gear on deck, they are soon broken off.

Grease nipples fitted in protected places enable grease to be forced into a bearing, which can reduce both corrosion and wear. They are usually fitted to bearings which work under pressure such as blocks, but all the other moving parts on a boat can benefit from lubrication. There are numerous small items such as door hinges and locks, the hinges of freeing ports, and window clamps which could benefit from the application of a little oil. Some fishermen hold the view that there is not enough time to attend to such maintenance and are prepared to let the various parts wear and seize up and that catching fish is more important. This is so but both can be achieved if maintenance is planned.

This does not mean that the boat is laid up once a week for maintenance. The margins in fishing are too small to allow that. No, maintenance can usually be carried out in the many odd moments which occur, perhaps when waiting to go alongside, waiting to unload the catch, or at sea, waiting for the next haul. There are many such moments of time and they can be put to good use if it is known what must be done.

When the boat is new, or even secondhand, go round the boat making a list of everything which will require some form of maintenance. The list

164

should include everything from greasing the threads on a shackle pin to clearing out a store and painting the hull. It will take a while to make such a list, but it is worthwhile because a list of everything that needs doing to keep the boat in good order is established.

This list can then be subdivided into those items which require daily attention, those weekly, then monthly, half-yearly and yearly.

Daily items could include such things as checking the engine oil and water, checking for fuel or water leaks and checking the hydraulic oil tanks, the sort of quick check which should be done before setting off to sea.

The weekly items may include such maintenance work as greasing the winch and lead blocks, checking the hydraulic system for leaks and checking the steering gear. Now the list becomes more valuable because if these jobs are to be done in the odd spare moments which occur during a trip, then the list can immediately show what needs doing. Without it, half the odd moments of time can be wasted thinking about what ought to be done, and then the less obvious jobs are neglected.

Monthly tasks can include the oiling of all the small items around the boat, perhaps changing the engine and gearbox oils and filters and checking over ropes and wires for wear and tear. These are the sort of jobs which can be done when bad weather or repairs force the boat to spend a day in port. This list will probably contain the majority of items, and it can even be sub-divided into those which can be done in fine weather and those in foul weather.

The six monthly and annual checks will cover such items as painting and maintenance of the hull structure. These may be done when the engine requires overhaul. Such overhauls should be on the list anyway, or when the boat is slipped or dried out for bottom painting. There can be a separate list of all those tasks to be done when the boat is out of the water.

The list should be as comprehensive as possible, so that nothing is left out, and each item should be ticked off the list when that particular part of routine maintenance has been done. In this way, it will quickly become obvious if some part is not receiving its fair share of maintenance. Space should also be left on the list for any defects which are found. Many of them will not be urgent and can be safely left until the next overhaul period, but if they are not noted they can easily be forgotten. These notes will also serve as a reminder for any spare parts which may have to be obtained before work can start, and this may save valuable time.

Much of the value of maintenance will be wasted unless the right materials are used for the job. With new products and methods becoming available it is hard to assess the qualities of each, but unless there is the possibility of a considerable saving in the time and effort given to maintenance, it is better to apply tried and tested methods. Greases and oils are fairly straightforward, with greases generally being of the type which is not easily washed out by water. The oil used for general oiling does not have to be of a high quality, and indeed old engine or gearbox oil could be used, but it may be dirty.

With paints, the choice widens and becomes more difficult. For ordinary painting there is the choice between ordinary enamels, polyurethane paint and epoxy resin paint. For anti-fouling, the choice is even wider, but in general the better quality paints will last longer. Much depends on the preparations and the wear and tear to which the surface is subject.

For the outside of the boat, provided that there is good surface preparation, then polyurethane paint is one of the best. It is very hard wearing and is particularly good for steel hulls. There are two types: those which are ready mixed and those which are supplied in two cans which have to be mixed together. The latter is generally the more durable.

For normal touching up work, an ordinary enamel is probably quite good enough. Even so the surface should be prepared adequately. A very high pressure water jet is good for cleaning the outside of the hull, as it will remove marine growth as well as loose flakes of paint. A steel hull should then be wire brushed and a wooden hull rubbed down with very coarse sandpaper, and a suitable primer applied to any bare patches before the finishing coats are applied.

At longer intervals the hull should be stripped down to bare wood or metal. On a wooden boat this allows the caulking to be dealt with if necessary, and the timber can then be treated with a preservative. Preservatives are now available which will dry quickly and can be painted over. After priming the wood, finishing coats, usually of polyurethane, are applied.

Steel hulls are sand-blasted to remove all old paint and scale and this leaves a surface which should be treated immediately before further corrosion starts. An epoxy resin paint is usually used on the bare surfaces, and after two or three good coats, anti-fouling or polyurethane are applied to finish off. This treatment should inhibit corrosion for a few years, but any break in this tough surface will allow it to start off.

Many are the claims made for different anti-fouling preparations and unless one is prepared to experiment it is best to use one that is known. Find out what paint other fishermen in the area are using and how it is working, because what works well in one area will not necessarily be suitable for another area. This anti-fouling preparation used must be compatible with what is on the hull already. It is therefore better to use the paint range of one manufacturer.

More care has to be taken with aluminium hulls in the choice of paints, in particular the primers and anti-fouling preparations. An etch primer is used to ensure a good bond with the aluminium and the anti-fouling preparation used should be one which will not react electrolytically with the alloy. Many manufacturers produce special paints for use with aluminium.

GRP hulls are a maintenance problem on their own. The material will not corrode or rot, but the laminate can start to break down if water finds its way in. This can happen as a result of some of the chips and knocks which the material receives in use. The hulls are protected as far as possible to prevent this. With a chip, the laminate underneath the gel coat is exposed, and in time, water will very slowly penetrate the laminate. The penetration will be accelerated if the boat is subjected to freezing temperatures because the tiny drops of water freeze and expand, thus opening up the way for further penetration.

Annual maintenance can cure this problem by grinding out any chips in the gel coat back to sound material and filling with matching gel coat. A deep scratch may need filling with resin and mat, but the gel coat is adequate for small chips. It can be rubbed down and carefully matched in.

Ferro-cement hulls, like GRP have the reputation for requiring no maintenance, but this is not so. Like GRP, ferro-cement can deteriorate if the surface is broken and water is allowed to attack the steel reinforcing. The treatment is much the same as for GRP: the affected area is ground clean and then made good, either with a cement mortar or an epoxy resin.

Ferro-cement hulls are normally painted both to improve their appearance and to give protection. A highly waterproof coating is desirable and this is applied after first wire brushing the surface to remove any salts which might prevent a good bond. An epoxy resin composition is best for these hulls, and the first coat should be well thinned with the special thinner provided to allow for absorption. This should be followed by two more coats of the unthinned resin before the finish coats of polyurethane are applied. New or repaired ferro-cement hulls should be left to cure for at least a month before painting.

Hull interiors are often far more neglected than the outside, partly because the finish does not show, and partly because of the difficulty of reaching many areas. Wooden hulls are best left without painting, except perhaps in the engine compartments. The bare wood is treated with a preservative and this can be followed by successive applications at intervals. Using a preservative helps to protect the timber and also allows its condition to be seen. The preservative is also easier to apply than paint. It should be sprayed under pressure and, because it soaks into the wood, it will tend to spread into the areas which cannot be reached directly. It should even be possible to reach the areas behind linings if access panels are fitted.

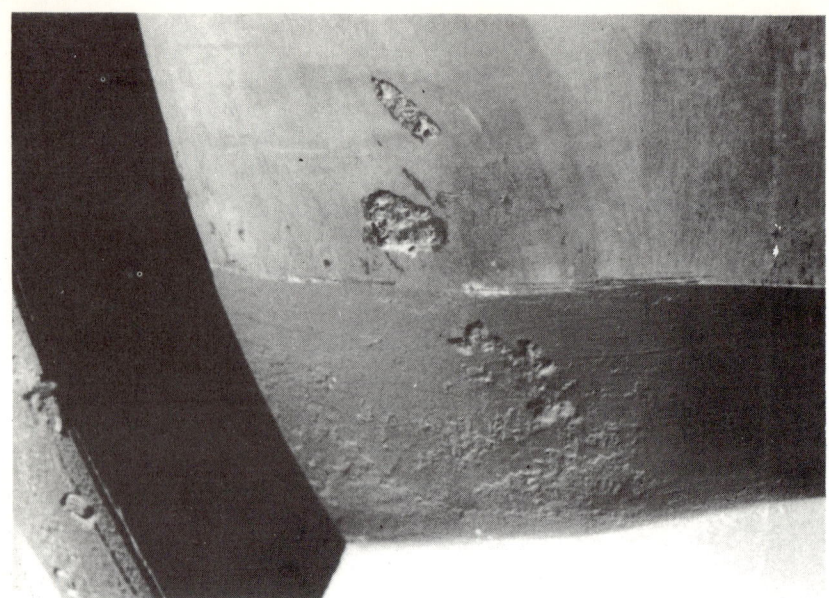

Fig 64   Chips in the gel coat of a GRP hull. Unless they are attended to, the damaged area will spread.

Fig 65   Complex fendering on a GRP hull. Maintenance of this is likely to be as onerous as that of a wooden or steel hull.

The wood preservative should be carefully selected, particularly for use in the fish hold area where it could contaminate the fish. Preservatives usually contain a fungicide, therefore the manufacturers should be consulted before using their product. The same applies to paints used in these areas. There are special preparations available for such purposes.

The timbers in the engine compartment are usually treated with paint to prevent or reduce the chance of oil soaking into the wood. White and light coloured paint helps to illuminate the area by reflecting light. Areas behind fuel tanks can be treated with preservative, but this does not protect the tank. This should be treated with epoxy resins as for steel hulls. Timber around hot areas such as the exhaust pipe should be well protected as they are vulnerable to rot. Protection from heat is important and the use of a heat resistant metallic paint can help.

Fig 66   The rot sets in. Decay in the join between the sides and the transom of a wooden hull. It should have received attention long before it got to this state.

The use of paint on structural timbers is not to be encouraged because a thick coat can conceal all sorts of troubles. At the first sign of rot, the affected timber should be cut out and if it is arrested early it will not affect the structural strength significantly. Impregnate the area with preservative and look for the cause of the rot. It may be damp seeping through from the deck or possibly electrolytic action. Damp is usually the cause and good ventilation is one of the best cures.

Steel hulls should last a long time if they are treated well at the start. Shot blasting and coating with epoxy paints will protect the metal provided the skin is not punctured. It is very difficult to treat the interior of the hull in the same effective way once it is in service, and treatment is restricted to the more accessible areas. These are the areas which are usually subject to damage of the surface coating so if extra care is taken when the boat is new the interior surface coating will last a long time.

The painting of the interior of GRP and ferro-cement boats is usually undertaken for the sake of appearance rather than to preserve the hulls. The areas where deterioration might set in are in the bilges, where water lies. Therefore a good sealed finish should be given to these areas, using specially formulated paints appropriate to the hull material.

The treatment of decks and working areas is always a problem. Wooden decks are best left in their natural state. Steel decks are often painted but this wears off quickly. This is not very important because the paint remains on the areas where it is wanted most. A GRP deck can be fairly hard wearing for normal traffic, but it is liable to damage if heavy fishing gear is dropped onto it. Many GRP boats have decks of GRP laid up over marine plywood. This provides a strong deck but if the GRP coating becomes damaged, water enters between the two layers which then rapidly separate and cause deterioration. If water does get into the plywood, then thorough drying out and resealing of the area must be carried out.

The treatment of the working gear is mainly covered by lubrication of the moving parts. If galvanized blocks and shackles are used, corrosion will be much slower to take effect. When such equipment becomes badly corroded they can be sent for re-galvanizing. For the smaller blocks and shackles it is worth considering using stainless steel. They will be more expensive initially but the maintenance required will be negligible.

Electrical equipment generally requires very little maintenance other than keeping it all clean and dry and servicing the batteries. This is always time well spent and special protective grease or a silicone grease spray on terminals can prevent damp and corrosion.

Electronic systems are generally designed to require the minimum of maintenance, and the handbooks supplied with the equipment will detail what is required. The main task is to keep the equipment clean and dry.

Aerials including the radar scanner should only be washed with soapy water. The rotating section of the radar scanner should never be painted nor the underwater transducers for the fish-finders and logs.

Engine maintenance will be detailed in the maker's handbook. Further than what is specified it is largely a matter of keeping everything clean and checking pipe clips, hoses and all the many small fittings so as to detect possible failures before they arise.

Good maintenance need not take up a lot of time. Over a period of a year it could provide several extra days at sea, days which otherwise have to be spent in port carrying out repairs. Maintenance need not be costly, but if done carefully and regularly it can maintain the value of the boat and lead to increased profit. Most important of all, regular maintenance can reduce accidents which are always expensive in terms of time, money.and personal suffering.

CHAPTER 14

Documentation

In the UK and other countries small fishing boats have come under the scrutiny of government departments. Fishermen must take a degree of blame for this because they have often been only too ready to flout authority, but much of the modern legislation concerned with fishing boats is intended to improve safety.

As much of this book will have shown, safety is largely an attitude of mind and is closely connected with first building the boat correctly and then maintaining it well. A large number of the accidents to fishing boats can be traced back initially to some fault on the boat and then the conditions at sea taking advantage of this. Probably equally to blame is an attitude which ignores defects in a boat, or a casual approach to navigation and handling with the result that a serious situation is not appreciated until too late.

Governments have to be seen to be taking action about accidents and the only way they can react is to make some rules which will, they hope, improve the safety. It is doubtful whether these have the desired effect because rules are unlikely to change attitudes. The effect on the fisherman of enforcing the rules is an added cost on his boat, which means that he has to fish harder and take more chances to make his boat pay its way.

Safety rules for fishing boats are by no means universal. At the time of writing they only apply to certain countries, but it is spreading and now IMCO which is a United Nations sponsored body concerned with safety at sea, is investigating the problem, and has introduced a set of safety rules for vessels over 24 metres. These rules at the time of publication of this book have yet to be ratified by the required number of countries and they are not likely to come into force for several years.

The lower size limit of these rules makes them inapplicable to the vessels covered by this book, but they point the way. Britain is one of the few countries to introduce safety rules for fishing boats below 24 metres. These rules apply to vessels over 12 metres in length. The British rules were introduced after a series of accidents involving fishing boats. The Canadian government is faced with the same problem and is considering legislation.

Other countries are likely to follow suit with or without the lead shown by IMCO. Governments tend to recognize that introducing legislation for safety does not immediately solve the problem. Safety is as much an attitude of mind as having a sound boat, but it is not easy to legislate for the former. Attempts may be made in the future to introduce more extensive legislation covering licensing of fishing boat skippers and crews, but at present the rules covering the fishing boats themselves give the fisherman enough to contend with.

However, rules are rules, and the fisherman will have to obey them. Unless the boat has passed its survey it will not be allowed to go to sea to fish. In the British system, the surveys are carried out when the boat is new and then at four yearly intervals, with a survey of the life-saving appliances and certain other aspects every two years. Not only is the fisherman faced with the cost of the survey, but he can also be faced with a considerable expenditure on replacements to bring the equipment up to standard.

The safety rules are very concerned with the stability of the boat and this has to be ascertained when the boat is new and at the four yearly surveys. This is done alongside by means of an inclining experiment, whereby a weight is moved about the boat and the change of heel measured. It can also be measured by means of a rolling test but this is not so accurate. To work out the stability from these experiments the naval architect must have a line and construction plan for the boat, so it is important to obtain and keep all this paperwork when the boat is new.

The boat is supplied with a stability book with all the relevant data in it. From this a skipper can work out how the stability of his boat is being affected by the catch being loaded or any other changes in weight on the vessel. The stability book will indicate any conditions of loading which may be dangerous and a skipper must make sure that the loading does not approach these parameters.

The survey covers the lifesaving and firefighting equipment and a separate lifesaving appliance certificate (LSA) is issued. The possession of a certificate does not mean that the boat is safe from fire or disaster. It only means that the boat has certain specified equipment on board with which to deal with disaster when it strikes. The same applies to the safety certificate: it only means that the boat meets certain standards of construction and equipment, and it will only be safe provided the boat is handled in a seamanlike manner.

Documentation does not end with a safety certificate. Most fishing boats have to be registered and have an identification number painted on the hull. This is necessary with the many restrictions placed on both the area and type of fishing and enables a boat to be easily identified at sea. There are certain advantages in having a fishing boat registered in terms of taxes and allowances, but these incentives vary greatly from country to country.

As greater control is placed on fishing areas with the introduction of 200 mile limits, licensing arrangements are likely to be introduced. By this it means a fishing boat will be licensed to fish in specified areas for specified species. Giving licences to fishing boats gives the authorities the means to control fishing in the interests of conservation. While the licences for fishing in home waters are likely to be fairly generous, those for fishing in the waters of other countries are likely to be much more restrictive.

Mention has already been made of the need for radio licences. Any transmitting equipment needs a licence, which is issued after the installation has been inspected and tested to ensure that it conforms with international regulations. These licences have to be renewed at regular intervals, unlike the radio operator's licence which has only to be obtained once. The operator's licence required on a small fishing boat is the restricted radio telephone licence which entails a simple test in the R/T procedures.

Certain sizes of fishing boats are required to have licensed skippers and engineers. The lower size limit varies from country to country, but because of this it is common to find large numbers of boats built to a size just below the limit. This puts an artificial constraint on fishing vessel size and the same can be said of the safety rules which at present do not cover boats less than 40 feet long.

This covers most of the official documents needed before a boat can go fishing. The list is formidable and is likely to increase in the future. In addition, there are certain requirements for navigation which common sense and, in some cases, regulations dictate.

A magnetic compass is not much use unless it has been swung and the errors of the compass tabulated on a deviation card. Even with a gyro-compass fitted, this is still necessary for the magnetic stand-by compass.

It is not possible to give a complete list of the documentation and certificates required for fishing. These vary a great deal from country to country. For instance, in the USA there are few restrictions on fishing vessels and the only safety requirements are Coast Guard recommendations. It is hard to see this situation continuing and the same applies to the EEC countries which are almost certain to follow the lead of Britain in introducing increasing legislation to cover both the construction and operation of fishing vessels.

International regulations require that a boat carry navigation lights and shapes constructed to certain standards. The sizes and power are laid down in the International Regulations for the Prevention of Collision at Sea, and one aspect of the new rules, which are directed at fishermen, is that the fishing shapes required by the rules must be taken down when the boat is not fishing.

No longer can all the fishing boats in harbour be festooned with balls and cones.

Because many fishing boats are built under a loan or grant scheme or even with money borrowed from the bank, the lender requires some assurance that the boat has been built to a satisfactory standard. Government departments lending money will usually make their own inspections by a specialist surveyor. Banks may insist that the boat is built to the standards of one of the classification societies such as Lloyds, in which case Lloyds surveyors will oversee the building of the boat. This can be an expensive operation and banks and other finance houses may often be satisfied with a report from an independent surveyor.

A surveyor's report is often demanded by insurance companies before they will issue cover on a secondhand vessel. There is usually no problem of obtaining insurance for a new vessel but it is preferable to seek firms specializing in fishing boat insurance because they understand the problems involved and are likely to be more sympathetic when claims have to be made. Few insurance companies will insure a vessel for its replacement value so a realistic valuation of the vessel should be obtained.

It is becoming increasingly important to cover a fishing vessel against third party accidents. These could amount to very large sums and insurance cover is the only way to reduce the impact of large claims. Similarly, the crew should be insured against injury or death.

Operating a fishing boat requires a wide range of experience in a variety of fields as this book has shown. It is not possible to be an expert in all of them and the skipper's job is to catch fish. It is hoped that this book will provide general guidelines as far as the boat and its equipment are concerned, but there are experts in many of the specialized fields who can go into specific problem areas. Fishing is a fascinating business, and as more and more government departments become involved the fisherman's job becomes harder, but the hardest taskmaster of all in fishing, is the sea itself.

INDEX

Other books published by Fishing News Books Limited, Farnham, Surrey, England

Free catalogue available on request

A living from lobsters
Advances in aquaculture
Aquaculture practices in Taiwan
Better angling with simple science
British freshwater fishes
Commercial fishing methods
Control of fish quality
Culture of bivalve molluscs
Eel capture, culture, processing and marketing
Eel culture
European inland water fish: a multilingual catalogue
FAO catalogue of fishing gear designs
FAO catalogue of small scale fishing gear
FAO investigates ferro-cement fishing craft
Farming the edge of the sea
Fish and shellfish farming in coastal waters
Fish catching methods of the world
Fish inspection and quality control
Fisheries of Australia
Fisheries oceanography
Fishery products
Fishing boats of the world 1
Fishing boats of the world 2
Fishing boats of the world 3
Fishing ports and markets
Fishing with electricity
Fishing with light

Freezing and irradiation of fish
Handbook of trout and salmon diseases
Handy medical guide for seafarers
How to make and set nets
Inshore fishing: its skills, risks, rewards
International regulation of marine fisheries: a study of regional fisheries
    organizations
Marine pollution and sea life
Mechanization of small fishing craft
Mending of fishing nets
Modern deep sea trawling gear
Modern fishing gear of the world 1
Modern fishing gear of the world 2
Modern fishing gear of the world 3
Modern inshore fishing gear
More Scottish fishing craft and their work
Multilingual dictionary of fish and fish products
Navigation primer for fishermen
Netting materials for fishing gear
Pair trawling and pair seining — the technology of two boat fishing
Pelagic and semi-pelagic trawling gear
Planning of aquaculture development — an introductory guide
Power transmission and automation for ships and submersibles
Refrigeration on fishing vessels
Salmon and trout farming in Norway
Salmon fisheries of Scotland
Seafood fishing for amateur and professional
Ship's gear 66
Sonar in fisheries: a forward look
Stability and trim of fishing vessels
Testing the freshness of frozen fish
Textbook of fish culture: breeding and cultivation of fish
The edible crab and its fishery in British waters
The fertile sea
The fish resources of the ocean
The fishing cadet's handbook
The lemon sole
The marketing of shellfish
The seine net: its origin, evolution and use
The stern trawler
Training fishermen at sea
Trawlermen's handbook
Tuna: distribution and migration